EDUCATION TODAY

Educational Revolution

EDUCATION TODAY

For a full list of titles in this series see back cover

Educational Revolution

JAMES CARMICHAEL, M.A., F.E.I.S.

Headmaster, Queen Anne Junior High School, Dunfermline

HUMANITIES PRESS · NEW YORK

Contents

CONTENTS

Preface

To pass brief comment on current educational change, assess its extent and indicate its directions are, perhaps, useful tasks but theirs is, inevitably, a transient satisfaction. Some way ahead must lie the more rewarding labour, the evaluation of those changes in the light of experience and research.

The changes which we witness have been variously sponsored. Some, for example, in curricula, come to meet the current explosion of knowledge and the new social needs of a rapidly moving society. Others stem from the experience and ideals of educationists, dissatisfied with past or current practice. Yet more come from political philosophies with their passionate rejection of segregation and stratification in school organisations.

Over all these brood the problems of our current economy, denying or delaying the resources necessary for the new educational environments required. We are, therefore, condemned, in some measure, to deny much of the present, to project hopefully a brighter future, but to creep forward when we would, most willingly, make haste.

No one can deny that there are dangers inherent in educational change. We are dealing, in the bodies and minds of our children, with the nation's greatest responsibility and greatest wealth. This is not a responsibility to be undertaken lightly. At the moment we press for change. We can hope that such change will be reform, but we cannot quote much more than experience of past frustration and good intentions for the future to support our claims.

There have been too many pilot schemes and too little controlled research employed in the initiation of our New Deal for Education. We have not tried sufficiently to effect, in terms of statistical appraisal, true comparisons between old and new methods and systems. We may, indeed, have missed great opportunities when, during the transitional period, when old and new systems ran concurrently, we did not promote research and evaluation.

Efforts to improve education are threatened, within the teaching profession, by extremists of two kinds. There are the die-hards, those whose educational arteries have long been dangerously hardened. There are, too, those who love change for its own sake and who value a reputation for modernity above the search for genuine reform. Add to those professional attitudes the social and political attitudes whose prejudices and tenets are entirely rigid and unassailable by the voice of reason or experiment. And we have some small measure of the difficulties besetting the educational worker who can never hope to disentangle his plans or changes from the society of which they are an integral part.

Current society faces a dilemma in its approach to Education. Parents see children enter new fields of knowledge by new methods and are bewildered and frustrated by their own inadequacies. Employers call for new knowledge and a new flexibility of attitude. Politicians see the hope for the future as depending on a new scientific revolution. Children appear to react in some measure against the drive for Science and Technology and students are, all too frequently, more interested in a new social order than in their contribution to the current one.

These questions must be answered. What do we teach? How do we teach it? How are teachers to be recruited and trained for a new system of education? Where should the education service rank, in terms of personnel, accommodation and equipment, in the national budget? To evade such questions is to strip naked and show, in all their puny weakness, the host of good intentions which marches across the educational stage.

Our plans for the future are full of challenge. Our hopes are high. Surely we have made plans enough, reports enough and an embarrassment of declarations. Let us be mundane and discuss resources.

I

Educational Change

The educational system aims to serve two needs, the needs of the individual and the needs of the state. The democratic aim is that every child should receive an education suited to his or her aptitudes and ability. The economic aim is that the fruits of education should contribute to the national wealth and wellbeing.

A survey of the educational scene shows advance and reform, real or projected, on every front. The entire system of primary education is under a process of revolution. In the secondary schools curricular revision, a new examination system, and plans to raise the age of compulsory school attendance to sixteen are all well under way. Further education colleges, often highly experimental in design and purpose, widely provide a new challenge to the school leaver. New universities are being established and are offering new courses and concepts to a wider band of entrants. Meanwhile, the older universities struggle with their younger sisters for the means to expand and modernise. Over the entire range public funds are sought in ever-increasing amounts to keep pace with new aims and projects.

It might appear at first glance to any foreign visitor that he witnessed in education the fruits of a bounding national economy. And yet we know that the reverse is the case. We are spending not for luxury, prestige or culture but for national survival. In educational circles we have awakened to the demands of a new and continuing industrial revolution. It may be that ours has been a tardy awakening. If this is so, the more urgent the need for modernisation and reform.

Teachers, often inward-looking academics, are sometimes

scarcely conscious of the forces and social pattern that drive them to change. They constitute no crack force to meet the tasks ahead. Too numerous to be well rewarded, they are too few to man the classrooms, workshops and laboratories. Short of money, we are still shorter of personnel. Other sectors of public services and the growing demands of industry for academic and highly trained recruits have denuded the teaching ranks of a growing number of highly qualified potential recruits. Gaps have been filled by recruits all untrained and too often unqualified.

The profession acknowledges the pressing need for change. Yet it must, understandably perhaps, approach such changes as a series of forlorn hopes. There are indications that morale is low, as witness the strident demands for status and the continual internecine war among teachers. There are, however, happier indications that the love of learning and the desire to serve are still vitally alive, as the generous response to limited inservice training shows.

The driving forces of our new age are curiosity and experiment, and the pattern of education is changing to meet these needs. The child in primary school will now learn by doing, by living experimentally in his environment. The secondary pupil must discard the old static Science–Mathematics and move forward in a spirit of exploration. Less academically he will learn by involvement and not passively by rote. Languages, now come alive and useful, are abandoning the overemphasis of the written word, too often taught in hackneyed patterns. The academic pupil must no longer study to get into university. He must prepare himself to continue his studies smoothly and without violent transition in university and college classes.

We have not, of course, and will not readily solve the many problems involved. When the educational sleeper awakes he does not readily adapt himself to new concepts and new values. There is, inevitably, a desire to repeat educational patterns. They make life so much easier by formalising knowledge, limiting the teaching remit and killing curiosity and experiment. One hears, too often, some one claim that he is 'too old a dog to learn new tricks'. There is a ripple of early retirement. This may well be due to exhaustion. It may equally be a confession of failure to meet current demands. Schools, colleges and universities are becoming big business, and big business is not for those dedicated to cottage industry.

There is, of course, a basic inconsistency in the national attitude to education. We need a national plan for transport, we are told, as also for power, agriculture, etc. But in education we tend to have no more than principles and aims, too much permissive legislation and too much persuasion. The modern secondary school may cost three quarters of a million pounds. Yet those who run and organise it are lifted raw from the classroom. No staff college exists, no managerial training to ensure the efficient use of heavy public investment. Now that we are awake, surely we should coordinate plans and train administrators.

At a time when the need for mobility of labour is paramount can we afford to leave education anchored to a series of parish pumps? We cannot ask workers to move here and there when by doing so they may ruin their children's education. One cannot defend chaos by calling it variety. The teaching profession is, it must be admitted, afraid of a national system of education. We have none the less to admit that the interests of children are paramount and must be served.

It is, then, most interesting to survey current change, to see its uneven effects, to see even the contradictions and curtailed opportunities. A cool look may not solve the many ills. It may, however, serve a useful purpose by acknowledging their existence, and by indicating possible surgery. British education is threatened by great difficulties. But no greater threat exists to both education and national life than the 'happy men' who resist change.

2

A New Order in Primary Education

It may be no exaggeration to say that our old and in many cases existing type of primary education has had one aim—to prepare for secondary school. The infant school target has been Reading, Writing—and basic number. This was followed by rote drilling in junior classes, while Primary VI and VII became a narrow and intense race towards the transfer examinations. It was the task of the child to learn, not to experience. Much good teaching did provide educational experience, but the serious business, well defined in time allocation, was to learn and prepare for the secondary stage.

Our reformers have reacted against this. They state that primary education is a separate form of education in its own right. This, while an understandable reaction, is, of course, an overstatement. Education must be and is a continuing experience divided only as an administrative convenience. None the less, no one will dispute the policy that children should learn and do learn best in situations challenging them to curiosity and experiment. This is not contemplated as a return to Rousseau's natural man. It is directed, rather, to let the child challenge his contemporary environment, where science and the scientific outlook are a normal part of human evolution.

What then is the basic task of the primary teacher? Briefly to create and encourage learning situations and then to guide pupils' efforts within those situations. This calls for new freedoms, far less sitting and listening, much activity and endless patience and versatility on the part of teaching staffs, acting both as individuals and as teams. Pupils, once set on exploration, will present an endless challenge to their teachers, a challenge which must be met.

Areas of desirable experience have been variously defined. They involve environmental studies, mathematical and scientific studies, and artistic experiences. If guidance is not given and if targets are not clear, the result could be a mass of ill-related knowledge with little common core. Throughout all work the teacher must maintain the steady learning process, encouraging effort and shared experience so that groups build up the necessary foundations of future educational progress. Substance must not become the victim of method, but more substance should be achieved by better method. We must have from the primary school a fund of necessary knowledge. We have too often had an array of facile tricks, numerical and linguistic, directed as a sort of magic to exorcise the evil spirit of promotion tests.

It is feared by the Old Guard in primary schools and the impatient specialists in secondary that the primary schools will now stop teaching, and that the children will have no measurable knowledge or skills. This is, of course, nonsense. The method is being improved. The content should be better known and not merely an examination façade.

Such methods have inevitably led pioneers of primary education into subjects which have normally been regarded as in the secondary reserve. A modern child experiencing learning must contact and become involved in mathematical concepts and scientific experiences. Such fields of knowledge are part of the natural environment. We cannot close such fields with notices marked 'Secondary only!' Similarly in language studies. The world is smaller, as children know both by viewing and visiting foreign countries. They see their parents attempting languages other than their own. Children want to join in—not, be it marked, as a grammatical exercise, but as part of a learning experience.

It will be tragic if such lively curiosity, aroused in primary school, is neglected in secondary. There must, across the ability range, be a moving together of primary and secondary education. Groups exist in primary school. Sets are simply groups in secondary. It is unfortunate that past traditions and snobberies, aided and abetted by the present Teacher Training Regulations, divide the House of Education into primary and secondary. Quite obviously it would be to the benefit of all if teaching experience gained across the whole front of education were subject to no training or promotion restrictions or financial penalties. These may be the consequence of scarcity—an obvious ruse to direct teachers into certain types of work—but the real sufferers from such policies are the children.

One cannot effect educational reform by edict or policy statement. It must be done by long and arduous effort. Alibis for inertia are ready to hand: lack of money, lack of staff, lack of accommodation, the need to retrain, and so on. All these are genuine disincentives. But the greatest impediment to reform is simply inertia.

To say this does not free the government and local authorities from their obvious obligations to invest in reform. They cannot hide behind good intentions and dedicated self-sacrifice on the part of teachers. But both sides of the house, must, above all, show willingness to go forward.

A real earnest of good faith would be a sensible attitude to in-service training. Teachers must be taught and continue to be taught to modernise their methods. Industry accepts gladly the retraining of personnel for greater productivity. Too many areas and administrations do not see education as our basic industry, where increased productivity gives better workers and citizens. A clear and planned directive is needed here. It is not enough to point happily to recruitment in vacation courses.

Primary reform, strangely enough, makes little or no reference to the preschool child, that stage where lasting and sometimes intractable attitudes are most readily achieved. Educationally and financially our children still do not exist until they are five, save in the field of family allowances. Resources are, of course, too clearly limited. But limited resources call for planned priorities. We await a firm policy declaration on priorities.

3

Transfer to Secondary Education

The area in our educational system to which parents and teachers alike have reacted most sensitively centres upon the transfer tests, the selection procedures which, at eleven plus in England and twelve plus in Scotland, have determined the nature and type of a child's secondary schooling. In Scotland, for some time now, an average of 25 per cent of children have been graded as suitable for senior secondary education in high schools. In England entry to the equivalent grammar schools has been attained by a number around 15 per cent.

Such rigorous selection has continued the educational and social prestige traditionally accorded high schools, most of which can look back to a past of still more rigorous selection and, indeed, to fee-paying on the part of parents. It is small wonder that parents have attached so much importance to the stage of transfer, when academic opportunity and social ambition united to strengthen their hopes. Success has been a cause of delight, and also of over-optimism. Failure has left a bitter inheritance of resentment and despair.

The teachers, too, have responded readily to parental pressure, measuring their own prestige and success in primary education by the number of children urged on to success in attaining senior secondary grading. Education has been narrowed and, indeed, too often forgotten in the cramming for transfer successes. Subjects not appearing in the test battery have been neglected or have received scant attention and little time.

The test battery on which the fate of children has hung has normally, in Scotland, involved a test battery of six marks. The two subjects tested have been English and Arithmetic. Two estimate marks have been given on school performance in those subjects. Two external test papers, one in English and one in arithmetic, have been given to the candidates. And two group tests of intelligence, sometimes called Verbal Reasoning Tests, have completed the battery. The marks were then scaled and the pupil given an adjusted average, a classification of singular potency. It must be added that comment on marks in such subjects as composition, social studies and tactile ability have often been added as additional information to transfer schedules, along with health and other details likely to affect a candidate's results. But, defying mathematical evaluation, such additional marks have seldom been a genuine element in grading. The consequences in written English have for long been painfully apparent.

How successful has past practice proved in educational grading? The tests have been heavily loaded towards linguistic ability, under the influence, perhaps, of the numerous language courses available in high schools. The element in the tests which has achieved the highest correlation with S.C.E. Higher results has been the interpretation passages in the English tests.

There was, for a time, a wide area of wastage in high schools, with many pupils leaving in fourth year. Partly to answer this the Ordinary grade of the S.C.E. was introduced in the fourth year of secondary education, to give examination results to fourth-year leavers and to act as an incentive on the way through school. This examination was also made available to pupils in junior secondary schools and in further education centres.

The results achieved in the Ordinary grade by pupils previously classified as 'non-certificate' have not yet been widely analysed but have been sufficiently great to destroy belief in the validity of the existing transfer test system. Socially, too, such results have induced an amusing dilemma. As high schools have been esteemed so junior secondary schools have been held in low regard, despite the fact that, less examination-ridden than their more academic fellows, they have been more experimental in outlook and liberal in policy. One might say that the educational worms have turned. Yet so strong is tradition in a race politically left and socially right that one often wonders if it takes a certificate of eight 'O' grades in junior secondary to match one of four achieved in a socially prized environment.

The important results of the 'O' grade have been two. They have shown that, in using the present transfer techniques, we have been unjust to wide areas of pupil ability. They have also posed the problem of how to reorganise transfer to secure justice for all children.

Two solutions challenged us. Would we reject the whole system of tests? Or would we, accepting the idea of testing, seek to achieve better grading techniques? Of those, the former has been accepted as being suitable to the concept of comprehensive secondary education, where, under optimum conditions, all children from a catchment area would enter one six-year comprehensive school.

At the time of transfer now it is recommended that joint consultation take place between feeder primary schools and the receiving secondary schools. The primary schools will submit all possible evidence on their entrants to secondary. There will then be an orientation period and a course of common content in early secondary education, organised, it is hoped, to meet each pupil's individual ability contours.

Such proposals are liberal and idealistic, but must also be recognised as posing many administrative problems. The new process will be extremely time-consuming at a time when curricular reform has made increased demands in subject time and set more challenging examination targets. There must be widespread experiment and patience while this is taking place. If we can attempt to achieve justice for all and combat socially divisive tendencies, we shall have done much, and our national life may well be healthier and our industry better recruited.

4

The Comprehensive Ideal

The comprehensive ideal of secondary education is now official government policy. And yet the comprehensive school has been, throughout debate, as ill-defined as it is ardently sought and opposed. Basically the aim is to educate all the children from a catchment area in one secondary school. Beyond this, organisational ideas differ and are blown hither and thither by the winds of political utterances.

England, with a long-standing and high tradition of very selective grammar schools has either attacked the grammar schools as being socially divisive or defended them as being the main bulwark of high standards of academic attainment. Scotland, with a large number of burgh high schools taking all secondary pupils, has been, initially, less alarmed by the proposals for comprehensive education. Parental support and opposition to the comprehensive system does not conform to social stratification. Supporters for the comprehensive school are to be found among all classes. Some supporters cherish its social ideal of a unified community, others see it as one way of solving the social and educational risks now involved in the gamble of the Eleven plus. The opposition seeks mainly to protect its children, already at grammar school, or to preserve the system of high grade selective education for the future.

It is when we turn from the basic ideal of a school for an entire community to details of internal organisation that the sparks really begin to fly. Those supporting the comprehensive school then urge entry without selection tests, now widely accepted, no streaming of classes into top, middle and low sections, and a common course for the early stages of secondary school education. Such proposals have exposed those Scottish schools claiming to be comprehensive as, in fact, multilateral schools, rigidly streamed, and providing separate systems of education for the able, the average and the less able. In extreme cases it has been found that such schools have, in fact, been a system of three schools in one, with the able pupils occupying a position of complete selective privilege and status, with corresponding loss to the average and below average pupils.

The teaching profession itself has been seriously divided on this issue, partly because of self-interest and privilege, self-interest and under privilege, and widely varying sympathies and beliefs. Teachers know that there are, in the most general terms, three broad areas of pupil ability, the 20 per cent able, the 20 per cent backward and the 60 per cent of so-called average, about whose lot the more sensitive consciences are troubled, notably following academic sucesses attained widely from this section. It is quoted that government policy lays down that each pupil should receive an education suitable to his or her aptitudes and ability. Some still maintain that streaming into above average classes, average classes, and 'modified' classes answers this need best. If this be so, then surely the multilateral system is best.

Such an attitude is indeed rough justice. It still clings to the idea of a small pool of ability in contradiction of the established fact of widespread academic success outside the area of the privileged elite. We have never really explored the educability of all our children and a main cause of this has been a system of rigid streaming, coupled with intensely selective staffing for the privileged few.

And yet comprehensive education, as a reform, has suffered less from its antagonists than from its supporters. From the doctrine of a clearly classifiable elite they have reacted to total egalitarianism, refusing to recognise that children do vary in ability. Such extremists advocate classes alphabetically selected, comprising all ranges of ability and, we are told, the social and educational millennium will follow. The vast majority of professionals deny this.

Nor has the Government found the implementation of comprehensive education an easy task. It has had to suggest that the first steps to comprehensive schooling be organisational, not financial. It has, because of the divided control of education, to ask local authorities to submit their individual plans for comprehensive schools—within, at the moment, existing buildings. It has hesitated before the built-in challenge of public, independent and grant-aided schools, and been attacked by both sides of the comprehensive argument for doing so. It has upset wide sections of the teaching profession by advocating and condoning centralisation into big schools, economically and educationally defensible, but death to a vast number of promoted posts in teaching. Unwillingness to create new mandatory promoted posts, really needed in the very large schools, has made teaching less attractive to ambitious recruits at a time of teacher scarcity.

In such circumstances, the local authorities do not have to look for their difficulties. Although all political parties support comprehensive schools in their utterances, some authorities resist the idea by various foot-dragging exercises. All look for a formula which will meet their building facilities and please most of their communities, while being acceptable to Government policy. The magic word 'flexibility' is at every level the talisman. The eleven or twelve-plus can go as a widely popular measure. Then variety becomes possible if economic arguments can be found to support it. We have now a rash of different 'comprehensive organisations'. Populous areas can frequently mount six-year comprehensive schools, if they are willing. Others follow such varied solutions as middle schools, bridging primary and early secondary schooling, followed by comprehensive senior schools: junior high schools, shedding able pupils at second and/or fourth year into selective high schools: area education systems, often stemming from the common campus schools of the North of England. Variety is the spice of life and it is both professional and British to resist uniformity. But what of the children?

We live in a time which encourages mobility of labour. This is a feature which the Government is anxious to promote. Yet the fate of a pupil moving about among such varied organisations must surely be a hard one. His education will be comprehensive beyond the intentions of any well-intentioned educationist.

Let us examine the implementation of real comprehensive schooling. It must direct its aims to secure three objects—the social integration of the community, the preservation of high academic standards, and the exploitation of every pupil's gifts to the ultimate limit within a six-year community.

The new transfer procedure will call for a period of pupil orientation. After this the school must provide classes as social units and sets for subject instruction according to the individual pupil's varying ability contours. The intitial course may be common, but it must be pursued at varying speeds and depths within sets of like ability. As the pupil progresses through the school he must be encouraged into the open-ended study of his gift subjects. The resulting fourth, fifth and sixth forms should bear witness to the full exploration of pupil educability.

Size of school, too, must be rationally limited, in recognition of the community's social needs. Much mathematical nonsense has been produced, by grossly overprivileged schools, in an attempt to blow up the comprehensive balloon until it bursts.

We must learn from the mistakes of others. The Americans favoured comprehensive education to create Americans. The Russians also followed this course to educate an illiterate population. They are now, their initial task completed, turning to intensively selective systems. With our standards and sophistication we can have both comprehensive schooling and high academics, if we really want to realise this aim.

5

Curricular Reform

In the late nineteenth century and early twentieth the educational system had three main objectives: first, the gentleman's education, largely cultural and moral, and directed towards the arts of government, at home and abroad. Next came professional education, for Church, law and medicine, the last of which achieved a belated respectability. The armed services also offered a traditional social status and an improving measure of training. Lastly there was basic education, training the operatives for industry. In Scotland's more democratic tradition it was possible, as proved by exceptional cases, to aim at and perhaps reach any career target. The Scots highly prize this tradition as being evidence of 'character'.

The spread of scientific knowledge and political democracy produced new educational targets and widening opportunity after the 1914–18 war, but postwar depression let this new liberty lapse into fairly rigid patterns, with limited thought, much rote learning and, of course, examination success.

Since the 1939–45 war science has burst the industrial, social and educational framework wide open and we now live in a welter of educational reform, as education strives to meet the new and ever-changing demands of industry, commerce and communications, all allied to a baffling social fluidity.

Secondary education is, of necessity, an affair of specialists. If you ask a primary teacher what he teaches, he will refer to his class. The secondary teacher will almost always name his subject. Reform of secondary curricula has therefore been conducted largely by panels of experts, that is people expert in a particular subject. This process has been vitalised and encouraged by Her Majesty's inspectors of schools, also specialists in the secondary sense. Much good work has been and is being carried out.

We have the impact of linguistics upon English study, the results of which may become more apparent when the linguistic specialists determine clearly their own aims. Mathematics is abandoning the merely calculative for the speculative, striving to achieve mathematical thought as opposed to mathematical gymnastics. The revolutionary thought has dawned that modern languages are for use, not merely for examinations, and it has also been noticed that most people speak more than they write. This concept has not yet been accepted, of course, in our native English. In the sciences, physics, chemistry and biology, a conscious effort is being sustained to arrive at hypotheses by experiment and then explore their further implications. The social sciences, history and geography, have been given a heave towards modernity by the introduction of a mélange of history, geography and economics, termed modern studies.

In technical and commercial subjects, subject content has been expanded, improved and related to industrial needs. Domestic science now produces meals which are not only edible but domestically sensible and garments which appeal to the tastes and age groups of their makers. In the realm of art there is scarcely a technique or skill closed to the ambitious student. Musical opportunity has been widely extended, although content usually remains haughtily classical.

We have left to the last the classics and Gaelic. How does one modernise the classics? Apparently by less insistence on grammar and syntax, a wider range of reading, more emphasis on the study of Greek and Roman civilisation, and, of course, more emphasis on the literary heritage of Greece and Rome. This, it must be admitted, is a bold struggle for survival. In Gaelic we have to cater for native speakers and those studying the tongue as an academic study. Here the struggle for survival has ardent supporters and romantic appeal. It is, perhaps, a pity that St Andrews House is in Edinburgh!

After such a survey one might say 'How wonderful! Surely all is well?' The answer, of course, would be 'No!' These reforming curricula tend to think downwards from the Sixth form. This has produced overstuffed curricula, now being slimmed. Again, much curricular reform has had to be made to think beyond rigorously streamed schools and into comprehensive education. It is so much more difficult to draw up curricula which exploit ability and yet offer transferability between sets. There is rife, too, an element of academic narcissism which has scant sympathy for lower levels of ability.

It is, perhaps, too early to comment on reforms in the curriculum, but there appears to be, as yet, little evidence that the new science/maths fields are proving more attractive than of yore. This hope may be realised, but only when the need to retrain serving teachers receives serious consideration. One can hardly keep pace with current change by attending, for a holiday fortnight, a college of education! Many pupils still remain painfully unimpressed by pro-science propaganda in choosing their future careers, while recruits to the New Age are more often 'stickit' than the divinity student of tradition.

We have, in fact, changed content but not changed student attitude. To do so is vital, notably in mathematics, where many a student feels an emotional repulsion to this study, a repulsion so common as to be widely sociably acceptable. We must, too, determine to let ability follow its bent. The school subjects are arranged in a hierarchy of esteem totally irrelevant to contemporary needs. Entry patterns into further and higher education should take a positive attitude to ability. Subjects need to be reassessed in importance in the light of their present day contribution. There are prestige subjects which have little or no current value, while others on which our present and future hang are insulted and debased. It appears that we cannot escape our past or accept that the majority of those in educational service are, bluntly, out of date in knowledge, method and philosophy.

6

Raising the School Leaving Age

It is the intention of Her Majesty's Government that in 1972 the school leaving age should be raised from fifteen to sixteen years. This intention has a mixed parentage. The measure was first promoted by a Conservative administration and is now a firm intention of the Labour Government, an intention held in the face of mounting difficulties and of certain professional misgivings.

Reasons for the raising of the school leaving age may be classified broadly as industrial and social. The spread of popular education has had, in the main, industrial motives. The first Industrial Revolution made it essential that the labour force of industry should have, generally, a basic education, and education has kept step, in some measure, with the growing demands of industrial complexity. This same industrial need is clamant today. We need a more highly and suitably educated industrial recruit. We are hit by scarcity in the vital technician grade in our industrial hierarchy. Still more, we need to shorten and intensify apprenticeships and to impress on all who work that they must be educated continuously for adaptability.

Social pressures, too, drive us to the extension and reform of popular education. Such pressures emanate from the speed of economic and social change, which affects both the individual and his environment. The more efficient our industrial organisation, the shorter the working week and the greater the leisure. The political scene, of unprecedented complexity, makes new demands on individual judgment. We live in a smaller world, where the national is being replaced, perhaps unwillingly, by the world citizen. And we live under the threat of catastrophe, a sophisticated situation where hysteria is dangerous and education must calm.

The raising of the school leaving age is not simply an extension of the traditions of current schooling. It must involve a new concept of education, in which school is only part of the general educational process. This process finds current, if sometimes disjointed expression in provision for further education, industrial training boards, in-service training, both industrial and professional and, a struggling infant, industrial re-training.

It is encouraging to note that, implicit in comprehensive education, is a new evaluation of ability where previously all prestige attached solely to academic ability. Work at all levels needs trained ability at all levels and, however narcissist intellectuals may be, their dependence on skills and knowledge, of both high and lowly order, is self-evident. For the industrial recruit his last year at school must provide industrial interest and motives, respect and praise for tactile intelligence and realistic education for the demands of a working environment. The school leaver should have experience of cooperative effort, not only in sport, but in workshop and classroom, and he must be subjected to the discipline of organised and shared tasks. Both the Brunton and Newsom Reports point towards such new ventures.

Alongside this, social studies in the extra year should introduce the school-leaver to the personal economics of paid labour, e.g. time-checking, national insurance, income-tax, banking, etc., and to the national economic framework within which he will work and to which he must contribute. He must see and be proud of the place of man the worker in society and be taught to appreciate the interdependence of all within modern society.

Education for leisure must be a vital element of fourth year studies. As leisure increases so those packaged entertainments, such as television and bingo begin to pall. Pupils would be greatly aided by training for active participation in leisure pursuits. Sports should be, increasingly, carryover sports, not those games which are generally abandoned by school leavers. Music, drama and crafts, the solace of reading, all should be part of the pupils' experience. It is to be hoped, too, that schools will not see themselves merely as starting points for such activities, but will become centres for youth efforts on those lines. Such a policy might go far to heal the major wound of our society, where the crudely termed 'teenager' is lost to the adult commuity during most impressionable years.

Education without ethics is merely a brutish and materialist pastime. Pupils can, surely, in a fourth year, be further involved in the virtues of responsibility and tolerance. Christian organisation may be attacked or ignored, but Christian virtues remain unassailed and fundamental to man's survival.

It is not enough to bear witness of intent, while ignoring the difficulties which beset the raising of the school leaving age. Those difficulties appear under one general and two particular heads. The general difficulty is economic, the finding of resources to build and equip school extensions, to staff them and to maintain the extended service. Much must depend on the view taken of this venture. If it is regarded solely as a social reform it may have validity, but its priority may be diminished. If it is regarded as an investment, the project must be so organised as to give assured returns in industrial reorganisation and prosperity. It cannot be enough to invest vaguely in the future, but both sides of industry must accept and deploy the new school leaver under different terms.

We must hope that accommodation provided will not be simply a matter of units, but will give a suitable environment for the new fourth year education envisaged, at least according to well conceived general principles, acceptable to pupils and educationists alike. The school of the future will remain in the future unless the educationist and architect cooperate. If we must meet cost limits it is reasonable to hope that this will not inhibit flexible and imaginative building. Without this, the reform will not be a reality.

The greatest problem, of course, is staffing. We cannot meet current needs; how, then, can we meet an additional burden? The hungry teaching profession is foiled in its recruitment hopes by other and growing national demands upon educated manpower.

There have been various moves to meet the situation. A remedy tentatively explored has been dilution, fiercely and understandably resisted, notably in Scotland. Now Robbins B.Ed. degrees offer a new, if limited, area of graduate recruitment. The new University of Stirling has projected and planned new specialist degrees with education: an academic course in which the student follows, simultaneously, basic and pedagogic courses. This experiment, if successful, may have many followers.

First among unexplored remedies is financial inducement. Despite improvement in teaching rewards and numbers, the great depression of the 1920–30s gave teaching its period of most successful recruitment. A second unexplored remedy has been a complete reassessment of the education tasks and rewards of the teacher. There is, too, a growing number of non-teaching posts for qualified teachers in education, an empire-building at national and local level.

7

Examinations

As the context and duration of education change, so inevitably must the examination system. Examinations, by their nature and by their desire to equate standards have, unfortunately, a restricting influence on education. Curricula, generous and liberal in content are, all too frequently, bent to serve examination needs. The teacher does not merely see his pupils as examinees but feels that he also is under continual examination when his 'results' are evaluated. He becomes the slave of the system and tends to teach pupils to 'pass' rather than to educate them. He feels little resentment towards this system as he is the product of it and all too frequently relies on his past achievements in this field for status, both within and outside the profession. He is further confirmed in this attitude by emoluments graded on the basis of his academic attainments, and not on his performance as an educationist.

It is obvious that pupils require some yardstick as to their abilities and performance. It is equally obvious that the teaching given the pupil is often confined to what can be measured by the yardstick. This weakness has been recognised, as we have seen, by the abandonment of the eleven plus examination in England and the twelve plus examination in Scotland. This examination selected pupils for grammar or high school entry, but it also clasped in a narrow vice the teaching given in the top classes of the primary school. It tried desperately to be fair, but, despite this, deprived able pupils of higher education and limited the education of all. Its heavy emphasis on linguistic ability was admirably suited to selection for the language loaded courses of the grammar and high schools, but less well suited to meet a national famine in the mathematical, scientific and technical fields. It used twentieth-century statistical methods to promote a nineteenth-century concept of ability. And it has gone.

Parental attitudes, partly educational and partly social, showed bitter resentment towards the eleven and twelve plus examinations, attitudes which have gained widespread support for comprehensive schools. This, of course, has been balanced by a bitter opposition to comprehensive schools from within the area of likely eleven/twelve plus success. This resistance has been and is both vocal and well expressed, a natural feature when one remembers that, in England at least, the vast majority of successful candidates for grammar school have come from the middle and lower-middle classes. It has been shown that children from such a social background and of merely average intelligence have enjoyed greater success in achieving eleven plus success than children of humbler circumstances with higher native intelligence.

Despite all this emotion, attitudes towards examinations in secondary and grammar schools have been much more quiescent. The examination systems applied in post-primary schools in England and Scotland have differed widely, in organisation, content and intent. The English system has been administered by nine examination boards, examining candidates broadly at the Ordinary level, and on an extremely narrow but highly graded front at the Advanced level. The Scottish system was, until 1964, administered by the Scottish Education Department. Here the leaving certificate, at both higher and lower levels was taken, until 1959, in the fifth or sixth year of high school education. Pupils leaving before this stage, left without nationally documented results, with only an unfinished course to commend them to employers. This area of wastage led to the initiation of the Ordinary grade of the Scottish Certificate of Education for fourth year pupils and the Higher grade for fifth and sixth year. The old idea of a group leaving certificate was abandoned and individual passes, graded as to quality, accepted. By this change the Scottish system embraced at the entry date to high school education, the top 30 per cent of the ability scatter. The English system is moving away with difficulty from a national average of 15 per cent of pupils accepted into grammar school education.

In both England and Scotland, however, secondary modern and junior secondary schools have enjoyed considerable success at the Ordinary level or Ordinary grade. The Scots have further followed the English pattern by setting up an Examination Board, established in 1964. Under this, practising teachers have much greater involvement in setting and correcting papers, a revolutionary innovation in Scotland where this work was previously discharged by the inspectorate.

It had been, traditionally, the Scottish attitude to see in its Higher Leaving Certificate evidence, equally valid, of general education or of suitability for university entry. The single subject pass recognition can, in many cases, scarcely testify to a general education and the preponderant influence in Scottish high schools is the university entrance standard. The control which this exerts on curricula balance, timetabling and subject prestige gives food for thought and misgivings, when one remembers that out of an average 25 per cent entry to high schools only 6 per cent attain university entry standards. Concern has been felt, too, at the high rate of first year university examination failure in Scotland. To remedy this, a Certificate of Sixth Form Studies is being introduced in Scotland. This is not to be an advanced level, so it is affirmed, but an examination to promote study habits, and to counteract the passive acceptance of vigorous teaching by Scottish pupils.

But what of the 80 per cent of English pupils and 70 per cent of Scottish pupils rejected by the academic examination systems? In a national system of education and against a background of employers seeking evidence of school achievement surely their efforts need some form of graded certification. The English answer to this has been the Certificate of Secondary Education, operated locally, but certificated nationally. This has been married in England to the 'O' level examination, by allowing the granting of 'O' level passes to those attaining high grade passes in the C.S.E. This, however, is not a 'marriage of true minds'. The examinations are so dissimilar that the passes granted at 'O' level are often more honorary than valid in content.

So far, the Scottish system has rejected the concept of an examination below the Ordinary grade. Perhaps justly, the Scots view the C.S.E. as an awkward and inefficient palliative. Yet this is of little help to the examinationally disinherited 70 per cent. There is a sense of grievance here which will become more vocal and urgent with the raising of the school leaving age. If we wish for a new relation with further education, employers and trade unions we shall have to revaluate the examination system.

Examinations, with all their faults, do try to give a measure, however inaccurate, of pupils' attainments. But the net is cast only for fish of academic weight. We must continue, at a time of rising academic and industrial demands, to fit pupils carefully for their future tasks. But we cannot do this by ignoring the vast majority, even if the teaching profession itself, rapt in academic slumber, may blench from a wider task.

To our mind the weapons lie ready to hand. The A level and Higher grades are the necessary measure for entry to academic careers. The 'O' level and Ordinary grade can, without loss, alter their functions and become examinations to grade the vast majority of pupils in their sixteenth year. To evade this issue is to promote industrial chaos. We can and do select our academic students. We can surely grade those technical and labour forces on which the existence of all depends. There has been much superficial change of organisation, some liberal and exciting change in the content of traditional examinations, but the whole concept of national examinations awaits urgent and revolutionary review.

8

Universities and Further Education

The British universities are, of course, now front-page news. The decorous days of calm announcements of appointments, scholarships and degree results are, at least temporarily, gone and we are striving, as in other fields of education, to finance a great expansion of university education. The recommendations of the Robbins Report reflected rather than initiated this movement and, indeed, it is now generally accepted that Robbins underestimated our needs.

This expansion has, as its main driving force, the belief that university expansion is vital to industrial expansion, a belief which provides, perhaps, an unhappy bedfellow to the older concept of the pursuit of learning for its own sake. We seek the expansion of knowledge, not as an end in itself, but as a contribution to the solution of econmic stagnation. The money spent is not regarded as a contribution to learning, but as an investment of public funds from which dividends are urgently needed.

The concept of complete academic freedom, still clearly held and doggedly defended is, in consequence, losing ground. The expansionist policy has made the position of the government, as paymaster, too strong to be seriously resisted, and the universities, like every facet of national life, are beginning to wear the harness of productivity. This has not been enunciated in particular terms, but the general point is well taken, even by those who resist it.

Our ancient English universities still enjoy maximal prestige and endowment, but they are conscious of the new mood. They are no longer the automatic first choice of English students and they see, quite clearly, that they must retain their prestige within a new concept of the university's contribution. Their long and distinguished history and their many privileges make it quite likely that they may adapt themselves, indeed are adapting themselves to change, more readily and with more sophistication than some of their 'red brick' colleagues. The spearhead of change is, of course, to be found in the new foundations, such as Sussex in England and Stirling in Scotland. The atmosphere of experiment, even in the organisation of courses, is extremely attractive to a youthful generation, as impatient of the past as it is of the present.

We owe much of the inspiration of current change to American educational philosophy, where a broader concept of the elements of university education prevails and where the use of graduates as growth points in industry is widely accepted. It has been, traditionally, our university aim to produce the educated individual, adaptable, confident and ready for further training in specialist functions. America, while admiring and copying much of British tradition, has given much more attention to the vocational training of the student. British industry has been slow to exploit graduate recruitment. This may well be due to an industrial desire for the trained man as opposed to the generally educated man. To those who see this as a failure to promote genuine academic challenge we have only to point out the Massachusetts Institute of Technology, where creaming and challenge can stand comparison with our British best, but where American society enjoys immediate profits from the education provided. There is less time to accept, train, and direct the charming confidence of the learned amateur.

There is one great area of concern which covers both schools and universities at present. We look for the economic fruits of educational expansion in the fields of science, mathematics and technology. Yet those are the very faculties which remain stubbornly underrecruited. New syllabuses in the schools have sought to stimulate career interest in the mathematical scientific field. Yet a disproportionate number of pupils and students turn away to liberal and linguistic studies. Propaganda has failed too, where students, encouraged and driven into scientific work, often constitute wastage there and turn to other careers. Perhaps a root cause of this student distaste for scientific work lies in mathematics. In relation to mathematical studies students fall into three categories, those who are mathematically gifted, those who are, at least, mathematically intelligent, and those who have no gift in this field. There is, unfortunately, little rapport between the gifted and other categories. It is as if the possessors of vision viewed, with amazement, the colour blind. We must bridge this gulf as the only way to combat the mathematical famine. The mathematically intelligent can contribute greatly to scientific expansion if they are not repelled by emotional attitudes deriving from unsympathetic instruction.

The Scottish scene differs widely from the English. The older Scottish universities, all ancient foundations, have only lately been joined by one new foundation in Stirling, two converted institutions, Strathclyde and Herriot Watt, and one separated college of St Andrews, forming the new University of Dundee. It may well be thought that Scotland, with its population of five million has been overprovided. But this is more apparent than real. Scottish university education has always been much more democratic in aim and organisation than has English. The foundations of this attitude stem from a democratic Church and national poverty. The upsurge of industrial prosperity in the Scottish midlands produced, not new universities, but the Royal Glasgow Tech. and the Heriott Watt College in Edinburgh, both striving to bridge the gulf between liberal and professional studies in the older foundations and the technological challenge of the new industrial revolution. But, if education recognises the demands of a new age, and economists urge upon Scotland, deprived of her heavy industries, the need to start new growth points, Scottish industrialists continue to underemploy graduate talents. The reorganisation of shipbuilding and the new computer industry may give a new impetus to the proper deployment of highly trained personnel.

In the universities we have, it might be said, assessed our problems. We have still to meet our urgent needs. Those who promote a 'two culture' war do little to aid either culture. If we are to educate the whole man, he must be a part of the community in which he finds himself. We must direct our intentions and energies to the academic concept of man in a modern, scientific and industrial community, creating wealth for survival and leisure for liberal pursuits.

A growing subject for concern, as university education is deployed before an ever growing number of students, is that of university wastage—the increasing number of students who sustain examination failure. We have still to establish the cause of this, and, of course, are given varying causes by those contributing to the students' education. The schools suggest that universities are preoccupied with research and neglect instruction techniques. The universities, notably in Scotland, counter by suggesting that school pupils are taught subjects but not taught to study with dedication. Those footing the bill for students' grants go so far as to suggest that some economic stringency might have a beneficial affect on students by encouraging plain living and high thinking. Students, in an apparently affluent society, suggest that they are already in financial straits.

There can be little doubt that university and school teaching both need attention at the transfer stage. To this end, the Scottish Education Department is initiating sixth form studies as a bridge to university. The universities must maintain their research priorities, to keep abreast of modern knowledge. They must, however, pay more regard to their instructional function. This task will increase as the intake net is cast wider.

Lastly, there is general concern at what is popularly known as the 'brain drain', the loss of brilliant students to America, where industrial wealth can deploy attractive research opportunities. Learning, of course, must be international if it is to be rich. Only a sound revival of British economy can increase the opportunities for British graduates. This revival would be greatly aided, of course, if those talents, now drawn to America were to stay in Britain and hasten an industrial resurgence.

9

Further Education

The growth of education in local further education and technical colleges has been extensive and rapid since the 1939–45 war. Further education is distinguished from university education by the vocational nature of its courses and diplomas and by its direct service to industry. We can therefore be encouraged by the massive expenditure which has led to expansion in this field, but rapid growth over very varying social conditions leads to an ill-coordinated system, and there is great need for coordination in this particular field of education.

There are marked differences between further education in Scotland and in England and Wales. This is only to be expected, as further education largely mirrors the industrial progress or decline of any given area. The massive attraction of industry to the south-east of England has greatly enriched the further education courses available in the colleges there. Staff in technical colleges in England is so numerous as to have its own association, the Association of Teachers in Technical Institutes. This body has its own publication on technical matters and is linked to the National Union of Teachers in matters relating to salaries and conditions of service. In Scotland the scene has been quite otherwise. Here further education at a high technical level has been largely confined to the industrial midlands with the marked exceptions of the north-east coast and the weaving districts of the Borders. The Scottish colleges have varied very much in quality and have tended in the past to be devoted to the one or two industries which characterise their particular neighbourhood. As Scottish industry has for many years been less prosperous and more volatile than English industry, so the educational contribution of the colleges has proved to be uncertain and of varying quality. This state of affairs has been well reflected when it has come to the staffing of Scottish colleges of further education. There the posts of high responsibility have frequently been filled by recruits from south of the Border where the ambitious had more ample means of improving their qualifications and experience. This influx, while educationally healthy, has had a peculiar side effect, in that there is a movement in our further education colleges to separate the teachers there from their traditional loyalty to older professional organisations in Scotland. It is not surprising that members of the ATTI, casting back their minds to the English industrial and educational scenes, tend to think that further education should be in a category of its own. Philosophically, of course, the departmentalism in educational thinking, which separates primary from secondary education and secondary from further education, is administratively convenient but educationally entirely unsound. One cannot but express the hope that education may be seen as a continuing process, which runs through all the types of schools, academies and colleges provided, and is then sustained by refresher and retraining courses throughout an entire working life.

The work of the colleges of further education has received a new incentive by the provision of the Industrial Training Act. By this Act a serious attempt is being made to establish standards of industrial training at a national level and to give a guarantee of proper training as opposed to the uncertain arrangements pevailing under the old apprenticeship system. While the colleges must welcome the provisions of this Act it must be pointed out that the demands of the industrial training boards sometimes take little heed of the normal requirements of college administration and staffing. It is quite easy for a specific board to make demands on college teaching time which cannot be met in terms of reasonable working conditions. One must, however, welcome any element of industrial reform and express again the hope that longer day school education followed by properly organised further education will lead to a general shortening in apprenticeships and an improved quality of training at the technician level.

Further education is close to the industrial soil of its various areas. It has not yet become a real national organisation and, indeed, may by its nature never become so. Nevertheless, efforts are now being made to investigate the organisation, salaries and conditions of service of teachers in further education. The Rogers Report conducted by the Scottish Education Department, after a prolonged investigation, tendered certain recommendations. This report was not easy to follow because its investigations were conducted into conditions bordering on the chaotic. This, in its turn, is easy to understand. The requirements of further education lead to a staff extremely mixed in qualifications and skills. Further education colleges must have their work organised to meet the needs of their pupils both part time and full time, and, therefore, hours of service can be debated. The promotion structures in further education cannot, as in day school, be built on any common denominator of qualification. Yet there is an intention, which we must welcome, to bring some definition and order into this most important sphere. This is a matter of urgency as a report on any branch of education directly linked to industry can swiftly become outdated by the movement of events.

Further education has to conduct helpful relations with the day schools and with industry, at both employer and trade union level. In the schools the Brunton and Newsom Reports are leading to a diminution of the traditional fear of any vocational element in general education. Indeed, new projects are being shared between the school and the college, and the raising of the school leaving age in 1972 would inevitably strengthen and broaden those projects. Relations with industry are more difficult for the further education colleges. It may be that a college will find itself preparing students for examinations and skills which industrial change has already condemned. Industry, too, is under tremendous pressure at the present time. There is a general need to modernise and further education must accompany any modernisation. There is a need in industry to reorganise and this may throw into further education another change in curriculum as skills and, indeed, jobs become irrelevant to the modern scene. The investment of industry in further education is moreover sometimes grudging and limited. Day-release in Scotland is poor when compared with the figures shown elsewhere. This is natural when one remembers that many Scottish firms are small and when one remarks the instability of the Scottish economy.

The changing industrial scene, however, where one must be efficient or perish, must lead to two movements in all further education centres. The first will be reorganisation and expansion to meet the needs of new industries and the second will be the relevancy of training given to growth points of new industry. It may well be that the further education college of the future will be of a campus design if lodged in a big industrial centre. Around this campus would stand the specialist departments, all of them related in work and inspiration to specific local industries. By this means the service given to industry will be made more efficient: also by this means the departure or collapse of any industry would merely affect one department in the college which can be rapidly adapted and organised to serve any incoming firm.

Further education moreover cannot escape from obligations for in-service training and in the retraining of personnel for re-deployment. It may be thought that separate centres for retraining unemployed would be enough to solve the problem, but the personnel who require retraining are not necessarily unemployed, and they can be best served if further education accepts the task of modernisation.

There must soon be moreover a revaluation of the curricula and status of the examinations for which further education colleges normally present. All people employed in education are unwilling to change well tried examinations but examinations must maintain their relevancy and one hears complaints in the most progressive sections of British industry that it is possible to achieve glory in further education examinations and at the same time to be gloriously irrelevant. While passing this stricture on further education one must also make it quite clear that industry has a duty to the colleges. In terms of reorganisation, high quality machines and skilled instruction many industrial firms have failed to keep pace with the colleges training their recruits. The college product may find himself or herself employed in conditions which cannot give scope to his training and skills. In many areas students are trained on firstrate machines to be employed on outmoded models. The only solution for this is the free and frank exchange of views. Further education boards are useful, as are all vehicles for informed discussion, but professional educationists are all too often in a minority. This may be the result of a feeling which has long existed between professional and business people but it is one which should be abandoned. The flight of public bodies from informed opinion, a flight which is not confined to this branch of education, is now entirely harmful to all progress.

The training of teachers for further education is now accepted as a challenge. It is at last agreed that a knowledge of one's subject is no guarantee of one's ability to impart of it. The arrangement for training teachers, however, is far from adequate and remains more of a gesture than of an urgent reality. One is further given to understand that the acceptance of training can have a peculiar effect on one's position in a structure composed partly of trained and partly of untrained personnel.

The overall picture is one of growth, expansion and excitement, but it is not yet one of good organisation, adequate training and overall modernisation.

10

The Teacher Organisations

In the public press teacher organisations appear generally on two unfortunate platforms, concerned respectively with salaries and conditions of service, and with breaches of professional conduct. If we turn to the educational press, we find teachers portrayed in an entirely different light, where they are engaged in educational experiment, in policy making and in reform. Despite the importance of the teaching profession as that laying the foundation of all other qualifications, its size and the greatly stratified nature of its qualifications inevitably militate against its remuneration. It shows, therefore, a picture of eternal complaint of which the general public readily wearies.

In England the main professional organisations are known as the Joint Four: the National Union of Teachers and the Association of Schoolmasters; affiliated to the National Union of Teachers there is the Association of Teachers in Technical Institutes; and beyond this there are the Headmasters' Conference (involving head teachers of schools recognised as public—because of their private nature), and similar associations depending on appointment and not election.

In Scotland, the oldest and most numerous teachers' organisation is the Educational Institute of Scotland. This is traditionally open to all Scottish teachers, has a Royal Charter and is authorised to confer the degree of Fellow. Its stated aims are the protection of teachers' professional interests and the promotion of sound learning. As a blanket organisation it is subject to the strains natural to a body striving to secure status and adequate rewards for all categories of teachers. It must achieve a balanced programme for teachers who, of course, see sectional interests writ large according to their various categories.

Upon occasion sectional interests have broken away from the Institute to form independent organisations. These interests founded the Scottish Secondary Teachers' Association in 1945, when the idea of a common maximum in salaries was temporarily promoted in the Educational Institute, and the Scottish Schoolmasters' Association, in which male interests felt themselves swamped by the larger numbers of women teachers. All three organisations share advantages and disadvantages. The breakaway organisations readily achieve unanimity for views expressed within them. They find those views correspondingly harder to promote in negotiations where small numbers and sectional views have to impress national bodies, who think of teachers collectively as teachers and who are impatient with teacher politics. The Educational Institute of Scotland has the advantage of representing a majority of Scottish teachers and of promoting the agreed policy of a cross-section of all teaching qualifications. Yet such a comprehensive policy inevitably represents compromise among many sectional interests, and, while compromise is politically inevitable, it is just as inevitably criticised by all who make concessions to achieve it. Yet the Institute is usually politically seen as promoting a balance of views and is consequently acceptable at the negotiating table. This, in turn, gives the Institute an 'establishment' aura, producing an automatic reaction from blither spirits. The S.S.T.A. and S.S.A. are frustrated in two ways. As 'rebel' organisations they find cooperation even with acceptable Institute policies to be embarrassing; and as small organisations they must push their representations *à l'outrance* to achieve results sometimes ephemeral. They must, too, attack the Institute, not only because they have sincere differences with it, but to establish their separate identities. Members of Parliament, living by internecine war, perhaps inconsistently regard teacher differences as unedifying, a view scarcely consistent with the general promotion of teacher interests.

In England, too, a similar scene may be witnessed. The National Union of Teachers is large, comprehensive and politically strong. A different salary structure and balance of qualifications in England lessen the tensions between teacher categories. The Joint Four, representing a grammar school elite have always accepted a heavy educational task, but have recently been, to some extent, bogged down in the prolonged debate on comprehensive education. When they come to terms with reorganisation their experience and academic strength will assert themselves as a major educational influence. The members of the Association of Schoolmasters are a fairly numerous body in England, but find themselves, as do the S.S.A. in Scotland, frequently a lonely voice, giving temporary cohesion to a varied opposition.

Despite the apparently schismatic nature of the teaching profession, all sections are genuinely interested in educational advance and reform. Their educational contributions are, to a great extent, conditioned by their political organisation. The large bodies, such as the N.U.T. and E.I.S. can consult their widely based memberships and see educational problems within the broad context of national educational interests. The smaller and more narrowly based organisations make specialist contributions of value, but inevitably lack close contact with the wider scene.

In consultation on educational policy with teachers H.M. Government strives to treat all teacher organisations without discrimination. Regard is given, within limits, to the relative numerical strength of the teacher organisations, but specialist bodies, e.g. the Headmasters' Conference in England and the Headmasters' Association (Senior Secondary) in Scotland, take equal place with bodies representing the great body of the profession. The result can be an imbalance of views and much vain repetition. Criticism is made that the popularly elected teacher bodies send politicians rather than educationists to educational consultation, but such complaints may be more convenient than real. H.M. Government tends to consult teachers within the context of nominated bodies, e.g. the Schools' Council in England and the Consultative Committee on the Curriculum in Scotland, and to promote experiment in selected schools and areas. Nationally, however, there is a wide area of consultation and agreement between major teacher organisations and H.M. Government. A notable exception to this may be the current policy on comprehensive education, but the method of introduction has sustained

36

more criticism from teachers than the principle. On the raising of the school leaving age teachers have endorsed the principle while querying the timing.

Consultations between teachers' organisations and local authorities are common enough but vary in quality and usefulness. In certain areas great harmony and unanimity exist, in others there is an armed truce, while too often the act of consulting is substituted for genuine consultation. And yet, with the current explosion of knowledge, and in the present atmosphere of experiment, teachers and employers are more and more encouraged to adopt agreed policies.

Interest in education is a link binding all the bodies representing teacher interests. It is far more important than the semi-political attitudes which divide them and it is in following their vocation with dedication that the teaching profession can win public esteem and true professional status. If the house of education is to stand it must lessen and ultimately eliminate its divisions.

II

Local Authorities in Education

Local authorities, within the national framework of education, build, equip and staff schools. They discharge those tasks under the general control of the Ministry in England and Wales and the Scottish Education Department in Scotland. In building schools their efforts, both in accommodation and expenditure, come under government control and they staff, as far as is possible, according to national standards of teaching qualifications. When they depart from such qualifications reports on such action must be sent to the Education Departments. In further education all appointments of staff must receive governmental sanction.

The control of education by local authorities is a historical financial convenience, as the large sums needed are borne extensively by the rates. Indeed, the burden of education on the rates has led both local councils and teachers to reflect whether the entire service should not be taken over by the central government. Local conditions in education reflect, more pointedly, national conditions. There are the same scarcities of money, labour, and teaching staff. Conditions vary greatly from one local authority to another, to such an extent that we preserve, only tenuously, the concept of a nationally efficient education service.

According to local authority attitudes and resources educational opportunity is far from equal throughout either Scotland or England. We can have one authority letting some 40 per cent of pupils enter certificate courses while another will be below the national average figure. National average figures differ between Scotland and England, 25 per cent into Scottish high school courses and 15 per cent into English grammar school courses. All

38

this is, of course, in the melting pot of comprehensive education. Yet in effecting a comprehensive policy for education the government again strikes difficulties created by local control. Such difficulties are ideological, where one authority will drag its feet in reorganising and another will behave with an enthusiasm which takes no heed of educational difficulties.

In staffing, too, local control emphasises difficulties. Attractive areas have no lack of qualified teachers, while socially deprived areas have their conditions worsened by the failure to secure teachers. To meet this problem quota systems and 'gentlemen's' agreements between areas have been tried, but not very successfully. There can be little doubt that local control militates against a national policy of teacher deployment.

Localities face vastly differing problems. Some areas house dying industries and conditions inherited from a more ruthless age. Populations vary and in many areas homes are still more important than schools. Standards of school building, while meeting national requirements statistically, yet vary tremendously in quality and suitability. In England there has been some attempt at intelligent expansion under a consortium of local authorities, but, so far, Scotland, where the industrial midlands cry out for such a scheme, has remained stubbornly backward. Local building policies have often been good and imaginative, but there has also been wasteful planning, unrelated to educational and national economic change. In relation to primary school building the national record gives an appalling picture, although some areas have been progressive.

To meet all those difficulties of administration and varieties of provision the current policy is to develop local government to cover larger areas. This would give such larger areas greater financial, structural and staffing flexibility and lessen the obvious contrasts existing now between wealthy and impoverished authorities. It might preserve, too, the advantage of maintaining the local financial commitment to education which the smaller areas find crushing. Much must depend on the geographical boundaries drawn. One can envisage larger areas where resources will still remain limited. We can hope for improvements from this plan, but not, perhaps, ultimate solutions.

Local councils are a traditional but peculiar part of our administrative system. They are popularly elected, but the electorate frequently neglects the polls. Their members are local people, well known and involved in their community, while M.P.s have to shuttle between Westminster and their constituencies. In education local councillors have to operate both local and national policies. Their attitudes are often buffeted by the contrary winds of national policy and local prejudice, as has recently been demonstrated by the application of the government's policy for comprehensive education.

Many people deplore the abandonment of the old *ad hoc* education authorities. These, they say, were composed of people really interested in education. This may have been so, but it is wrong to assume that education committees of county and city councils do not have a similar interest. If they appear less forthcoming this may well be because they see the educational provision within the general framework of local services and seek to serve in terms of reality—notably economic reality. There will aways be complaints regarding the running of services where political ideologies are involved. The medical profession has shared this experience.

It appears obvious that lay bodies controlling professions need the close cooperation and advice of their professional employees. This can be effected at four different levels: by the setting up of local consultative committees, by the co-option or election of teachers to council education committees, by *ad hoc* committees constituted for specific problems, and by consultation with the head teachers and staff whose work is being altered. Practice, as usual, varies between counties and between areas. In England and Wales teachers have for long appeared on education committees, but this change is being slowly introduced in Scotland, where some of the largest councils still resist change. It is amusing to note that local representatives, who welcome such innovations as the Clyde Shipbuilding Consortium, where trade unions and employers join to plan and advance productivity, still remain opposed to teacher participation in the local planning and administration of education.

Local consultative committees, too, can be greatly or marginally effective. Sometimes such committees are effective while in others consultation takes place but has little or no effect on policy. *Ad hoc* committees are generally effective for their specific tasks but make only a temporary and individual contribution to local government policies. Consultation with head teachers and staffs concerns the means of implementing, not the making, of decisions.

The central government is far more liberal in achieving joint programmes with teachers than are the local authorities. But no doubt these difficult days for education will enforce cooperation at all levels. The trend is in this direction and will be produced by men of good will working for the common good. It is fair to add that teachers, both as individuals and as representing organisations, need involvement in local government work. In isolation their views can often be unrealistic and their professional competence wasted.

The Ministry of Education and the Scottish Education Department could influence local authorities much more than they choose to do. Their approach in urging reform is too often permissive. Yet one must say on behalf of local authorities that they have a genuine interest in and personal knowledge of their areas. Centralisation of educational control would have certain advantages, but current opinion deplores centralisation and favours area control.

12

Area and National Educational Patterns

The variety of educational provision in Britain is both interesting and a cause for concern. The attitudes of local authorities make a great contribution to this variety, but there are areas of difference of wider extent and greater homogeneity. At a time when devolution and the relaxation of central controls are receiving serious consideration it is worth while to reflect on the educational attitudes and organisations which already control sections of the country.

The greatest demarcation line lies between the Scots and English systems of education. In education, as in Church and law, the Scots pursue an entirely different path from the English and Welsh. The Scottish system is based on the Scottish Office at St Andrews House, Edinburgh and is one of the many responsibilities of the Secretary of State for Scotland. National education is zealously guarded in Scotland for three main reasons. First, the Scottish system has always been more democratic than the English, stemming, as it does, from a church democratic in organisation and rendered literate by religious practice, that is by individual study of the Bible. Secondly, the remaining entirely Scottish institutions in Scotland are the repositories of national sentiment, and they resist interference, however well intentioned, as a national affront. Lastly, Scotland, as a poor country, early valued education as an escape from harsh circumstance and for a long period housed one of Europe's most efficient systems of national education.

The maintenance of the broadly based ordinary degree in

Scottish universities (a very different degree from the pass degree in England) is one reflection of an educated democracy. The larger number of entrants to grammar school education in Scotland, an average of 25 per cent as against one of 15 per cent in England, again indicates a wider concept of educational opportunity. The higher grades of the Scottish Certificate of Education, taken over a broad front and at a standard between that of the English 'O' level and 'A' level, secure a wider band of advanced schooling for Scottish pupils. The ancient Scottish universities are married to this system by the regulations of the Universities Entrance Board, where broadly based entry requirements have scarcely been ruffled by some relaxation in the entry requirements of the newer Scottish universities.

But, despite the merits of the Scottish system, it has found itself embarrassed in a variety of ways. There has been a considerable anglicising of the direct grant schools in Scotland, i.e. schools run independently of the Scottish national system, with the aid of government grants. Such schools increasingly cater for both Scottish and English university entry qualifications. State schools, too, are joining this trend, influenced by the pooling of university places over Britain. And it is, of course, inevitable that the educational opportunity offered by Oxford and Cambridge should prove attractive to able Scots.

In social organisation, too, the Scottish state schools have adopted an English nomenclature, at least, for aspects of school life. The appointment of prefects was taken up in the 1920s and house organisations have come in with a wide variety of interpretations. It has been both amusing and instructive to watch the reactions of the Scottish and English systems of education to the introduction of comprehensive education. A majority of Scottish burgh high schools have been traditionally comprehensive in intake, but rigidly streamed in organisation. Where junior secondary schools existed the Scottish attitude has been to look down on them, not socially, but academically. And certain Scots, at least publicly, argue against comprehensive non-streaming in terms of defending academic efficiency. In England the academic argument has also been widely used, but the social argument and the liberty of the parent are also war-cries there.

The Scottish universities have had an increasing number of English recruits. In the early university classes English students with 'A' levels enjoy an advantage over the native Scots, a dangerous advantage when many Scots university Faculties use the 'A' level standard as a starting point, and when merit certificates, gained in early classes, are a *sine qua non* for entry to honours courses.

The relationship between the S.E.D. and Scottish teachers is an infinitely closer one than that prevailing in England between teachers and the officials of the Ministry. There is a variety of reasons for this. The relatively small numbers involved make for intimacy. The teaching profession in Scotland has a heavy graduate intake to its secondary schools, and can consult with the S.E.D. on terms of parity. Teacher involvement in national policy has long been accepted in Scotland and is a reality, not a political gesture. Lastly, the inspectorate in Scotland has adopted, after a dictatorial past, a policy whereby it leads the teaching profession in urging reform. There are, of course, areas of confrontation where political solutions for which the S.E.D. is advocate meet with resistance from Scottish teachers. Yet it is seldom that common ground cannot be found to effect solutions at least tolerable to both interested parties. This may, of course, appear a flattering interpretation of the Scottish position. Against it, one must remember that the Scots are, essentially, schismatic, and the teaching profession frequently weakens its effectiveness in bargaining by internal struggles.

In Wales, which has no separate educational system to act as a vehicle for national sentiment, there are again marked areas of difference, in attitude and tone, from those prevailing in the English scene. Welsh teachers are often passionately nationalist in sentiment and, in Welsh speaking areas, dedicate their energies to the preservation of Welsh language and traditions. There is, too, a tension in Welsh education, stemming, as it does in Scotland, from the urgency to succeed when opportunity is limited. Here, again, learning is sought, sometimes to the detriment of liberal values. A very large number of Welsh students still turn to teaching as a career. This is helpful to recruitment at a time of national scarcity, but can have its dangers by the inbreeding of ideas. One

44

might wish that students from all areas should be encouraged to pursue their careers well away from their home districts and loyalties. Where regulations hamper this they hamper a liberalising process.

England, the most influential educational area in Britain, reflects a class-conscious community. It is accepted in England that the best education is at present provided by the public schools, which are both private and financially and socially exclusive. There seems little chance that, despite the Public Schools Commission, any fundamental change in this system is likely. There will be compromise, of course, but compromise in terms of continuing privilege with broader intake. This might appear wholly bad, but it should be remembered that public school education represents, within its social shell, the liberal concept of educating the whole child. It succeeds in this, of course, only in varying degrees, but the success of all systems is variable.

The English grammar school, too, accepts much that is fundamental to the public school philosophy, if we discount the boarding element. In terms of academic attainment against currently accepted scholarship targets the grammar schools enjoy great success. But there is, both in the public and grammar school position a weakness which cannot be evaded. Can systems be really effective which are enjoyed against a background of deprivation and socially divisive attitudes, which are housed in a no-man's-land across which the forces of private liberty and public weal face one another?

Across the entire English system, however, there prevail many generous and characteristically English attitudes. There is less tension in English classrooms, notably in the junior schools. There is a sense of greater freedom than exists in Scotland and Wales. And the end product is, perhaps, less formally learned, but more confident in the exercise of his talents than is his counterpart in the North and West. The ideal educational system, the teachers' New Jerusalem, would take the best of all three attitudes and achieve greatness.

13

Governmental Aims and Problems

The first task of H.M. Government in relation to education is to find the financial resources for its provision and expansion. In turn, the state expects the educational service to feed industry with recruits who will improve the national economy by their training and efforts. Thus, while sympathetic to education's more liberal and social aims, the government must give priority to those aspects of education which make a direct contribution to the national economy.

A marked result of this understandable attitude has been the emphasis placed, in recent years, on scientific and technical education in the secondary schools. As we have seen, scientific curricula have been overhauled in all branches of science. Mathematics, too, has been reappraised in content and modernised in approach, and technical subjects, at one time a repository for the non-academic pupil, are achieving a new status and undergoing a detailed study, both in scope and curriculum. Pupils have been and are under pressure to select courses involving a strong scientific element.

And yet, as has appeared in the Daynton Report, the pupil response has not been encouraging, notably in England. Scots senior pupils, with a broader target for university entry, show better distribution between arts and science subjects. Yet there are indications, in the lower forms of Scottish secondary schools, of a drift towards arts and away from science. There is little for our comfort in this, as our wealth depends on scientific effort and our educational provision depends on our wealth.

Why should this happen? It would appear to stem from two main reasons. Another governmental function is to ensure an adequate supply of properly qualified and trained teachers. This has not been achieved, notably in the vital areas of mathematics and science teaching. Secondly, industry has been allowed to drain off a greater and greater part of the university output of mathematics and science graduates. And where home-based industry has failed to offer opportunity, America and the Commonwealth have been more than willing to entice graduates to emigrate. Hence the public concern about the 'brain drain'. It must be remembered, too, that the number of students remaining at university to engage in research has been greatly augmented. In mathematics the teacher scarcity has reached the dimensions of a famine.

The arrival of such recruitment conditions can scarcely have come as news either to the government or to the teaching bodies. In science and mathematics we have, in fact, been eating our seed potatoes. Graduates, rightly aided by public funds, are becoming a form of public subsidy to industry at home and abroad. The universities, too, in pursuing their research commitment, in itself vitally important, have, in some measure, deprived themselves of future student recruitment into vital faculties. Government intervention in university policy would be, of course, regarded as an infringement of academic freedom.

And yet the government could take more positive action to maintain teaching standards, while encouraging the universities in research. There is no reason why research students should not be simultaneously trained and employed as teachers. A greater transferability, too, between industry and teaching could be actively encouraged. Presumably the universities wish to continue to recruit science, mathematics and engineering students. They can do this only if a sufficient number of graduates prove willing to enter teaching. The same applies to industry. It has a real stake in ensuring that graduate output is maintained.

The government attitude is to see an overall scarcity of graduates against a growing demand for their employment. Teaching requirements form a major section of this demand. The government therefore seeks to reduce demand in this large sector to effect an overall saving. To this end governments have striven to reduce the acceptable qualifications for teachers and to secure the better deployment of the teaching force. No government has accepted that a teaching career should be financially competitive.

An attempt has been made and is currently being made to secure the acceptance of new qualifications for teachers on the basis that such qualifications would not be inferior but 'different'. This argument does not bear factual scrutiny. There is little doubt that currently accepted qualifications vary in their relevance to the teaching task. There is a clear case for more relevance in qualifications, but no case for lower academic standards for teachers. The welcome afforded by teachers to Stirling University's new approach to teacher qualifications indicates that teachers are not backwoodsmen in protecting an academic *status quo*.

One must, of course, remember that no government is a free agent in its approach to education. Government aims include the extension of nursery school education, the rehousing of primary education, the improvement and extension of secondary education, and a wide extension of universities and central institutions. But the possible conflicts sadly with the desirable in terms of resources and labour. Where governmental control can be faulted is in its failure to plan and establish priorities. This is no easy task and is rendered more difficult by the power of the local authorities, a power conceded as financially convenient, but often proving wasteful when set against the national scene.

Where government attitudes have been helpful is in establishing new curricula and in encouraging new building design, although government influence in the latter can alienate the practitioner by a reliance on optimistic statistics and amateurism in projected organisations. And, of course, if one improves one's curricula one cannot make do with less well qualified staffs. Educational reform, too, dear to teacher and administrator alike, has, in current circumstances, all too frequently an air of unreality. It can involve the deployment of personnel and resources which currently simply do not exist. It can, moreover, when conducted by specialist panels, cause a time war between different interests and departments for an unrealistic share of the school timetable.

The revolution in education has been and is the outcome of individual advances by the varying subjects. There still remains the task of producing a coordinated and well planned structure for secondary education. At the moment the path to chaos is being well paved by uncontrolled good intentions.

In contrast to the apparent unwillingness to control and pattern subject balance, there is ample evidence of increased governmental intervention in the actual running of schools. This has stemmed largely from the policy of comprehensive education. The eleven plus in England and the twelve plus in Scotland have been abandoned under governmental fiat. Consultation between primary and secondary, an ill-defined procedure, takes the place of those examinations. Direction is given that the first two years of secondary education should provide a common course. The choice of subjects and examinations beyond the second year is becoming increasingly a matter for parental choice as is examination presentation. The balance between liberal and examination activity is being presented without overmuch regard to conditioned attitudes among parents and teachers.

And yet it is only fair to add that governmental attitudes are invariably attacked by professions. If they are rigidly patterned they are charged with being reactionary and illiberal. If they are progressive they are creating chaos. Teachers react to educational change according to their intelligence and their arteries. The case-hardened meet change with early retirement. The limited teachers find that change can often reduce their apparent classroom effectiveness.

As never before H.M. Government is anxious to encourage education relevant to national needs. This offers a great opportunity for advance and reform, but teachers must not expect such changes to be painless. It may well be that, in addition to in-service training for existing teachers, there must be a complete revaluation of teacher qualifications in terms of relevancy.

14

Parental Attitudes

Parental attitudes to education have varied historically to reflect the social conditions present. In illiterate and primitive societies learning was venerated, the teacher occupying a priestly role. Even when feudalism set some order in European society those complexities which called for literacy and numeracy were largely discharged by members of the clergy, although popular education sprang up with the growth of trade. Even this popular demand was met by church schools.

When feudalism began to creak and collapse the attitude of the masses towards learning turned to one of violent distrust. It seemed to the dispossessed that learning, as an apparent instrument of law and tyranny was to be distrusted. The pendulum swung some way from this with the Reformation and Renaissance, but the distrust lingered on.

With the Industrial Revolution came two concepts which were to win popular education real regard based on self-interest. First, the new industrial magnates needed some basic education for many of their employees. Secondly, it became possible to use education to scale the industrial and social ladder. The masses of the industrial poor, living in perpetual insecurity, saw in education a means of escape for their children. Reacting against their own harsh circumstances they strove themselves and made their children strive to use education to better their lot. This attitude was prevalent until after the 1939–45 war, and is by no means abandoned.

Whatever the stratification of society, be it feudal, aristocratic, plutocratic or democratic, education has always had, for parents, social as well as academic significance. Education was, for a very long period, a class privilege. When education was organised on popular lines, separate systems were maintained on class lines, for example, the public and independent schools. Such schools have offered and do offer, in many cases, an excellent education. When we had an Empire they trained imperial administrators. Now there is a move towards the challenge of business management at top level. In parental eyes they have social merit, as indicative of belonging to a certain social class and they are regarded as easing entry into influential spheres in business and society. They are unpopular and popular among parents. For some they are a traditional right, maintained in the face of growing financial difficulties. For others, they are a goal desired for one's children as offering both good education and the stamp of social success. By many they are bitterly resented as being a privilege bought to the detriment of poorer children whose state schooling offers, in many areas, limited opportunity and no social cachet.

Parental attitudes to state education currently reflect our new society, which has been termed the best informed and least educated to date. Education is news and parents are bombarded by news about teachers, schools, and schooling. News, of course, contributes to information in varying degree according to the organ presenting it and the person receiving it. Under National Health medicine patients have a right to treatment, but a right to a cure is another story. So in education pupils have a right to the best possible schooling. How far they will profit from this depends on their aptitudes and abilities, and, to a recognisable extent, on their domestic environment. It has been found that, in grammar school education, children of merely sound ability, but of literate domestic environment, have a greater educational success potential than children of outstanding natural gifts from homes offering no educational stimuli. Can parents be told that their children's one disadvantage is their home? Obviously not, but steps can and should be taken in school to redress this disparity by organised and supervised prep, and by study and social facilities. In education as in all branches of state service there is a parental preoccupation with the individual's rights. This is natural when one considers how hardly won those rights have been. But there is often apparent a declining attitude to parental duties to children. This has been exaggerated by the wealth of school opportunity now freely deployed and by the increasing number of families in which both parents work. Their children are all too often denied nothing materially, but are not given either the encouragement or opportunity to study.

The centralisation of schools and their growth into very large organisations is, apparently, an economic and academic necessity, but it has done nothing to improve the position of schools in the community. The wide catchment area does not see the school as a social centre, as was once the case. Parent-teacher organisations can be effective, but only if parents attend, and attend to cooperate. Members of large teaching staffs tend to become less well known to parents, and parents less willing to approach and consult the large organisation. Every effort must be made to counteract this and to establish opportunities and resources for parents and teachers to work together educationally. Such occasions may have their social and welfare aspects, but it scarcely seems advisable or professional that parent/teacher cooperation should be conducted in a prevailing atmosphere of sales-of-work, fund-raising, and tea.

Parental attitudes to teachers are both varied and peculiar. It is quite common for male parents to boast of the harshness of their early schooling as reflecting their early manly qualities, and to deplore quite mild disciplinary measures applied to their children. Again, well-meaning and sensitive parents attack teachers who resort to corporal punishment, but seem indifferent to certain parental behaviour, as evidenced by the growing brutality to babies, which gives hospitals widespread concern. At the other end of the scale a growing number of parents, apparently unable to control their young, are frankly willing to hand over all discipline to the school and, indeed, to afford teachers powers which are, naturally, quite unacceptable to them. The vast majority of parents, entitled to courtesy, consideration and acurate information, respond admirably and cooperate well. Their chief cause of concern has recently been changes in school curricula which leave them out of date, but enlightened efforts are being made to keep interested parents in the educational picture.

Teacher attitudes to parents, often sympathetic and understanding, can also be irritable and petty. Teaching is a difficult and trying profession, involving, as it does, constant contact with the unruly young in circumstances of seclusion. It is the ideal of the teacher to be fair and unprejudiced. To him the parent too often appears both unfair and prejudiced, unfair in asking for academic targets beyond his child's reach, and prejudiced in refusing to accept disappointing realities. It is a humorous comment on human nature that no section of parents is more prone to just those faults than teachers themselves. It is extremely hard for academic parents to accept limited academic talents in their young.

The teacher must extend his compassion beyond the pupils to include the parents. He must welcome natural parental concern, which reflects desirable interest, and strive to direct that concern towards the child's profit and happiness. Where parents are indifferent to children's futures he must encourage and inform them, and wean them away from an unambitious stance based on the current illusion of easy affluence. All this is greatly helped if teachers are willing to engage fully in society. Cloistered dedication has its admirable aspects but it involves too narrow a concept of the educational task. To advance learning in a social vacuum is to practise an irrelevance.

15

Pupils' Various Lives

All school children lead, to some extent, three different lives, often with three divergent sets of values. These lives are the life of the home, the life of the school, and the social life of their contemporaries. At an early age these lives show a reasonable measure of synthesis or, at worst, tolerance, but with the advent of the preadolescent and adolescent stages pupils are pulled in various directions and their school performance and social education enter a difficult phase. To take a simple example, pupils from areas of marked dialects early become bilingual, speaking at home and with companions the local dialect and at school some version of standard English. They then, at adolescence, acquire the prevalent teenage jargon, varying according to location and fashion, but deliberately withdrawing from their elders, both at home and school, and, indeed from younger members of their family.

This linguistic symptom is indicative of deeper changes in basic attitudes and emotions. After the 1939–45 war adolescent youth, all over the world, deliberately withdrew itself into a separate band in social life. This process has, of course, been seized upon by rich business interests, notably in popular music, clothes, publications, and entertainments, and has been fed and committed to continuation.

Much reporting is given to declining home influence, usually with adverse comment on the lack of parental control. But sympathy should be felt for parents facing a new problem in youthful revolt, the problem of organised separation. Children have always rebelled, consciously or unconsciously, against their parents, but have done so in recognisable terms based on values at least comprehensible to those parents. Now parents and teachers both find themselves rejected in terms of values beyond their understanding and often outside the range of their tolerance. Organised religion faces the same problem, often with the same sense of frustration. The indignant parent is a historical figure, but the frustrated and despairing parent is now regrettably common.

It is true to say that parents and teachers alike are less adequate than they were, even when we acknowledge the widespread loss of once valid traditions and faiths. Prevalent materialism and relative affluence have marred the adult moral sense. There is a general tendency among parents to provide gifts rather than guidance, and to converse of material success rather than ethical standards. Teachers, working within the social texture of their time and within examination laden curricula, tend to teach rather than educate. To teach is a hard task, but how much harder it is to educate. Teaching is so important, too, when the explosion of knowledge provides so many tempting targets. Yet this very knowledge needs educated people to handle it or it can become a wholly destructive force. We have ample evidence of the growth of intelligent and successful crime, if we need to hear a warning note.

Parental discipline falls too often into two categories, one repressive, the other acquiescent. Account of this has been taken in the Kilbrandon Report, involving the coordination of social services and work and the proper reinvolvement, under guidance, of parents with their erring young. But the benefits of this blueprint for a better future are being withheld. The reforms will cost money. They will also deprive jealous vested interests of power. A tragic feature of democratic institutions is that power once given to the inadequate is jealously guarded. Teachers are, naturally, in favour of such social reform, but their influence with local authorities is limited and, in some areas, denied. Yet teachers have the benefit of contact with children and can and must do more. School can be the bridge between youth and adult living and bear more of the burden once accepted by the home. To point out parental failings and do nothing for the children except discipline them in school and teach them is to deny to teaching an adult approach to current needs.

The most common beginning of delinquent tendencies is truancy. It must be remembered that the truant is adrift from both school influence and home influence. He has made his first antisocial gesture and probation reports tell how speedily graver consequences follow. School refusers, often the victims jointly of school subject difficulties and parental ambitions, tend to keep to themselves. Truants, on the other hand, seek the company of their like in rejecting discipline in its broadest sense. In hard cases there evolves the pattern of truancy, probation, approved school, Borstal and prison. Many are stopped on the way, by the dedicated efforts of teachers and social workers, but some inevitably complete the pattern as surely as other pupils proceed to university. And such cases can be recognised quite early, although adequate means to stop the process are still withheld. The lay attitude to truancy is both careless and sentimental. Kindly men and women do not want to get boys and girls into trouble. That is not their privilege. The boys and girls can manage this for themselves.

It may be that the increased social responsibility shown by housemasters and housemistresses in our large comprehensive schools will infect the profession. It may equally be that parental responsibility will become a genuine topic of public concern and not a privileged position held too often by the unworthy.

How does the teacher set about meeting the new challenge of the withdrawal of youth? First he must decide his priorities and determine to educate. He must interpret adult living and social activity in realistic terms, emphasising the social contract within which free men and women must live. In facing social problems youth can be brought to face his own. The teacher must break down the barriers which isolate him. If one asks a teacher what boys and girls generally want to be, he might say, with some truth, motor mechanics, and hairdressers. Both want, in real terms, to be married and have children. Yet we do not talk with them of marriage, children, and homes, of hire-purchase, of housing, of decorating, of rents, taxes, saving and so on. We talk to them about sex. Here we give them the facts in biology and the ethics in religious instruction or ethical talks. But the real need is to put both facts and ethics into their social framework of the home.

So also in relation to work. Teachers going out into factories and workshops to further liaison with industry often report adversely on work attitudes and an ignorance of taxation, insurance, unemployment, trade unions, and time-keeping. What recruits should know, first and foremost, is the place of the worker in society as the source of wealth and as a vital link in a complex chain of industrial organisation. We teach the history of the industrial revolutions and the history of the trade unions. It is surely more important to know of one's task in current circumstances and the grave measure of one's responsibilities.

The adolescent can escape from adult society and responsibilities only for a little while. The school must direct its efforts to preventing total disengagement and to preparing, in practical terms, for the inevitable reinvolvement in acceptable and happy conditions. Revolt in youth can still sponsor reform and memories of difficulties given to parents and teachers can contribute to wiser parenthood. Even the values of the present day, if interpreted in terms of human responsibility, can regenerate the ethical and spiritual life of our society.

16

The Recruitment and Supply of Teachers

Educational reform and progress rely, in the final analysis, on an adequate supply of trained teachers. Till this has been assured all liberal recommendations have a quality of unreality which can do little but produce cynicism within the ranks of the existing teaching force. The reformers appear to suffer from delusions like those which haunted Hitler in his decline, when he moved divisions on his war map—divisions which did not, in fact, exist. While the recent postponement of the raising of the school leaving age was made on economic arguments, the teacher organisations had already sounded a warning that, in terms of staffing, this reform was not yet possible.

Teacher supply has never been satisfactory in quality or number since the days of industrial depression in the 1930s. Then widespread unemployment and hardship made a teaching career attractive in terms both of security and of emoluments. Schools were flooded with a supply of teachers offering high academic and teaching skill and, indeed, unemployment was widespread among teachers. Schools were run by minimal staffs, and often with poor accommodation and equipment. Pupils, in terms of quality teaching, never 'had it so good'.

With the prolonged boom after the 1939–45 war and with the postwar population explosion circumstances in teacher recruitment changed dramatically. Many attractive alternative occupations in industry were available to graduates and the civil service and nationalised industries offered wide avenues of opportunity.

Teaching, too, lost its brief attraction in terms of finance, when graduates sought opportunity rather than security. While teacher salaries and conditions improved they none the less became unrealistic when compared with earnings attainable in other fields. Within the context of full employment and an affluent democracy the position of teachers declined and they became conscious of a loss, not only of earnings, but also of status. The honoured concept of teaching as a vocation lost its appeal, particularly when used by successive governments to stimulate recruitment within a falling market.

Successive governments found themselves in a position of peculiar difficulty. They had stimulated employment demands in the public sector and depleted the force of teachers. They accepted that the public sector of employment, notably in such a numerous force as the teaching profession, could not compete in financial rewards with industry. Yet they were and are conscious that their aims, both in industry and in social services, demanded an improved and expanded education service. This dilemma has not yet been resolved. The teaching force has been expanded but has not kept step with growing needs. Great sums have been spent on building schools, but, notably in the primary sector, a further colossal expenditure lies ahead. It has always proved more attractive both to governments and local authorities to build rather than to staff. Good buildings do help education, but the staffing shortage remains fundamental.

To meet the shortage crisis large numbers of uncertificated persons have been employed as teachers, persons ranging from the surprisingly adequate to the pitiful. Such people offer no guarantee of standards and their employment is bitterly opposed by teachers, both for the damage they can do to children and for the insult to a learned profession which they personify. It is difficult, too, for employers to present teaching as a status profession while they employ such people and the effect on regular recruitment is scarcely beneficial.

England and Scotland, having different educational traditions, have different concepts of teacher qualification and training. The Scottish universities produce large numbers of ordinary graduates while the English universities produce few pass graduates and emphasise the honours degree course, taken in three years beyond the school advanced level G.C.E. standard. Beyond their ordinary graduates, who have a three year course beyond the Scottish S.C.E. Higher, the Scots take a fourth or fifth year to secure honours degrees.

The colleges of education in Scotland are large and area based. They produce teachers for primary school and train teachers with university, technical or aesthetic qualifications for secondary school work. Until recently there was no primary course for non-graduate men in Scotland, but this has recently been introduced, a step which worries many Scottish educationists.

The English colleges of education, with important exceptions, e.g. institutes of education, are small and vary greatly in quality. They train large numbers of men for work in both primary and secondary schools. Much excellent training in teaching techniques is given, but, to Scots eyes, the basic academics required are limited.

The Ministry of Education and the Scottish Education Department have launched prolonged campaigns to recruit teachers. Against every disadvantage they have had some success in the college trained general subjects field. The Scots expect to meet their primary needs in 1968, a statistical success which, perhaps, ignores deployment difficulties. In the field of secondary education current needs cannot be met and the raising of the school leaving age lies ahead.

Thus, in secondary education, the uncertificated teacher continues and deployment studies are made in the hope that trained teachers may be better and more profitably distributed. In England the graduate teacher need not attend a teacher training college, but can learn by doing. The Scots accept this in further education colleges, but encourage in-service certification by financial inducement.

The effort to redeploy teachers can expect limited success only at the recruitment stage and may need financial inducements. To run schools on establishments argues a mobility which is a civil service and not a local government concept. Faced by Treasury cuts in all services, the government dilemma is a cruel one. To teachers it appears that what is wanted is better and extended education on the cheap. This is, no doubt, a limited view but one supported by the economic difficulties of young teachers.

A General Teaching Council is being set up in Scotland to give the teaching profession a larger measure of self-government. This body is to advise on recruitment to the profession and to discipline its members, ultimate authority resting, of course, with the Secretary of State for Scotland, representing H.M. Government. In the eyes of the teaching profession throughout the world the Teaching Council represents a great advance to a long-sought ideal. Yet its early steps in Scotland have been faltering and slow. It has endorsed the recruitment of college trained men for primary schools, to the disappointment of many teachers. It has secured consent to a policy to eliminate uncertificated teachers from primary schools, a problem really solved by an increased supply of entrants, but failed to secure anything but a suggested future date for a like policy in secondary schools. Further threats to its own continued existence lie ahead if H.M. Government should suggest dilution of secondary teaching qualifications.

It may be that inadequate teacher recruitment can be solved only by three major reforms. First, it may be necessary to set up a Royal Commission to establish education's staffing needs, in quality and number, for the next twenty years. Second, the problem of deployment must be settled in a way satisfactory to the teaching profession. Third, H.M. Government must have a clear view of the place of education in society and be prepared to meet that need in terms of financial investment. Teachers have to live and raise their families within the context and values of current society. If H.M. Government wishes to recruit teachers it must attract them. If it wishes educational advance it cannot have this against lower teacher qualifications.

I7

The School as an Organisation

The elements in school organisation are the economical yet fruit-
ful deployment of staff, the provision of generous courses and
liberal activities for pupils, and the full exploitation of the accommodation and equipment available. The actual education and
curricula available are, at any given time, largely dependent on
the availability of qualified staff, equipment and accommodation.
Schools have been, traditionally, given great liberty as to how
they organise their systems of education. This has been due,
partly to a liberal policy of trusting the man on the job, and
partly to the impossibility of making more than general recommendations against the widely varying conditions of individual
schools.

Accustomed to the traditional system of primary, junior secondary, and senior secondary school in Scotland and to the parallel
system of junior school, secondary modern school and grammar
school in England and Wales, head teachers have made the most
of acquired expertise in their different spheres. Now, however, all
are in the grip of disquieting change. The Plowden Report in
England and the Primary School Report in Scotland have
loosened traditional patterns in the junior and primary schools.
The talents of staff, working as teams, and the interpretation of
education as an experience rather than a quiescent and receptive
process, have made new demands on flexibility in organisation.
The targets of the eleven plus in England and the twelve plus in
Scotland are being withdrawn and teachers are having to rethink
and retrain to meet new educational targets and new processes of
pupil assessment.

In secondary education we witness the marriage of secondary modern and grammar schools to produce the comprehensive school which has been accepted politically as national policy. Such a marriage does not merely bring together two school organisations; it involves two separate educational philosophies and traditions and two widely diverse areas of staff experience and skill. The more unwilling partner is, as might be expected, the grammar school, and the more willing the secondary modern. The grammar school fears loss of prestige and, frankly, privilege, while the secondary modern hopes to acquire esteem and share privilege. These attitudes are generalisations. Certain traditionally selective schools show a firm intention to preserve standards and to expand their area of success within a comprehensive framework. Other secondary modern schools of high professional competence fear that much of their best work may be threatened by the favouring of an academic elite within the comprehensive framework.

Be this as it may, school organisation must now meet the challenge of the comprehensive. Such an organisation may expect to be large, as small comprehensives, indeed small secondary schools are, we are told, uneconomic. It is regrettable that there is no firm definition of the term comprehensive to guide innovators. Its main aims are flexibility and width of educational opportunity and social integration. To achieve these aims we are told that pupils should not be 'streamed' and that the first two years of secondary education should consist of a 'common course'. It is also recommended that the large school should be divided into houses, which may be organised within specially designed accommodation or organised without physical framework. Those houses are designed to reintroduce that close personal and social contact with pupils against which size may be said to militate. Existing comprehensives, introduced under the Attlee Government, have been run largely on the setting principle, that is each main academic subject has been taught in subject groups of like ability, with the free movement of pupils up and down sets according to their performance. This follows the group method long practised in primary schools which, of course, have always been comprehensive. Now, however, we have the advocacy of mixed ability groups as the teaching units in the first two years. It must be noted that, while many support this arrangement in general terms, they find it impracticable with the most gifted and least gifted pupils. There are no results at accepted examination levels to approve or discredit this practice. And the question of possible change in examination targets has not yet been answered.

There must obviously be an interim period of organisational trial and error. Education cannot afford a leap into the dark, but must accept change within the conditions that are best for pupils of all categories. An interim organisation appears likely to accept the following lines.

The common course, taking in pupils who enter secondary school on the basis of primary school reports, must be regarded as, initially, a period of orientation. This period may be prolonged or shortened according to the validity of the reports received from primary schools and to the reaction of pupils to new secondary subjects. From orientation it seems likely that setting will evolve, a setting which will remain extremely flexible until every allowance has been made for the varying profiles of individual pupil success.

To achieve this will require simultaneous block timetabling of age groups within departments. This can both strain and ease the use of accommodation and equipment. It can cause strain by launching large numbers of pupils simultaneously into school departments, although this can be overcome by double-decking the subjects. Against this, it can secure the full use of departments, notably in practical subjects, where there has been some criticism of expensive equipment standing idle round small numbers of pupils.

At the end of two years pupils may be expected to have determined, by performance, their areas of academic potential. But this does not ease the organisational problem. In following their established patterns pupils outside the high academic range require accommodation suitable for the deployment of tactile intelligence and prevocational interests. Such organisation, too, must be timetabled to coincide with the non-certificate activities of certificate pupils, who must be encouraged to accept, without examination commitment, leisure activities and interests which will ensure a liberal education.

In certificate courses it seems likely that the Scottish and English systems of secondary organisation will move towards each other. The Scot will specialise more by attempting fewer subjects, while the English pupil will specialise less and attempt a more balanced curriculum, notably beyond the 'O' level stage. Sixth form studies in Scotland will require more careful timetabling than has been witnessed since the old interest in Bursary Competition work has received less financial incentive, while the English 'A' and Scholarship level work must answer the call for liberalisation.

House organisations can be organised either horizontally or perpendicularly. Where a two-tier system of comprehensive education exists, some schools form houses horizontally, by year groups. This is an administrative convenience but precludes many of the advantages of the perpendicular organisation, with its opportunities for competitive work and for house committees practising a measure of self-government. A great problem in older schools is the question of area space for house meetings and activities, as well as proper office and record facilities for housemasters and housemistresses.

There must, in transitional arrangements, be much thinking and practice. This is inevitable when education is faced with generous principles and restricted provision for their accomplishment. One would like to see patterns evolve rather than be imprinted, lest we lose the enriching qualities of variety and experiment.

18

School Buildings

The period following the 1939–45 war has witnessed a great expansion in the school building programme. This was necessitated by an upsurge of school population, caused partly by the birth rate and partly by the raising of the school leaving age from fourteen to fifteen. Additional causes were the expansion of senior secondary education and the need to replace buildings which had long outlived their usefulness. The halt to school building during the war and the limitation of care and maintenance due to war priorities, left a wellnigh insoluble problem for postwar governments, notably in the area of primary or junior schools, where the situation remains far from satisfactory. Recent events, such as the projected raising of the school leaving age to sixteen, the policy of comprehensive education, the new concepts of primary education, the introduction of new secondary curricula, and the expansion of further education, have all immeasurably increased the problems of school planners and strained the limited resources now available for school expansion.

There have been, as might be expected, very unequal degrees of success in meeting current problems as the local authorities have varied widely in their resources and in their willingness to promote educational building programmes. Two interesting contributions to planned expansion have been a general policy of centralisation and the functioning of a consortium in England using largely standardised and factory produced materials for school erection. Where the policy of centralisation has been belatedly undertaken, authorities have built schools which they can scarcely justify in terms of rational centralisation. And, of course, while centralisation may be rational, it has social disadvantages and has often been resisted by areas demanding their 'own school'.

While many fine schools have been built in recent years, it is true to say that the planning of schools suffers from various lasting drawbacks. The first of those is dual control, as exercised by the local authority and the government department. The local authority has to have a programme, but this programme is subject to changing policies and priorities and to central control, both architectural and financial. Again while many enlightened authorities are willing to be informed and guided by the professional advice of teachers, others are not. Such consultation is recommended by H.M. Government, but it is not mandatory. It is axiomatic that architects and teachers must collaborate if schools are to be really effective as instruments of education, but this does not always take place. One must, of course, pay tribute to those architects who accept the educational challenge and seek to familiarise themselves with the needs of a living school. But such attitudes and practices should be standard, not optional. School building means great expenditure. It is normally necessary to economise, but, even in the areas of economy, educational opinion is a valid guide as to priorities. It cannot be overemphasized that schools are not merely accommodation, but are rather an educational environment to give effect to academic and social aims.

Obviously planning teams should be set up in all areas, teams on which the cumulative experience of the teaching profession should have weighty representation. Teachers, too, must learn to think architecturally, just as architects must think educationally. It will always be necessary to get down to square feet and costing, but in the dispensing of public monies everyone accepts that the best possible buildings are all that can be expected, not the realisation of academic dreams divorced from reality.

It must be remembered that there is no harder task for the school planner than the constantly changing nature of his terms of reference. Population changes, due to industrial expansion or mobility and curricular changes to meet new educational advances may make a school out of date during the period covered by planning, costing, approving and building. Then we have the indignant taxpayer asking why 'new buildings' are so quickly inadequate. We live in an era when to modernise a factory is economically sound but to modernise a school is, all too often, thought an unnecessary financial burden.

Many school buildings, approved in their recent planning, are now regarded as containing wasteful elements. At a time of economy, 'dead' space, that is accommodation used only minimally, is rightly criticised. Such criticism finds ready targets in large school halls, repeated in many schools, and in large dining facilities. Such accommodation does stand empty for the greater part of each day. It is now suggested that school concerts, plays, and other public shows could be provided for in one central hall, for the use of schools in a given area. The cafeteria service of school meals has shown how dining facilities can be dispersed into dual purpose areas. Sports halls, too, can be more effective and widely used than duplicated gymnasia, and indeed, can be used for house activities, all-weather sport, and extra-mural clubs.

It has been felt, too, that at the top end of secondary education full classroom accommodation and laboratory and workshop facilities are often deployed against minimal numbers. Two suggestions are made to meet this: first, the inclusion of small rooms which can be used by small study groups and, second, timetabling which will fill rooms and allow group teaching if varying ability groups are so housed. The suggestion of small room provision is reasonable, but such small rooms will often stand empty and, indeed, take the place of the extra space unused in large rooms. Again, timetabling, now facing growing demands for block booking, is not as flexible as is often believed. Indeed, timetables are suffering from too many demands made by special interests, each devoted to their specialist needs.

Our American friends have evolved a more practical approach to structural flexibility by the introduction of movable partition walls running freely on rails. Such walls can be moved quickly to match the timetable pattern. There remains, of course, the problem of desk, seating, books and equipment, all of which must limit the effectiveness of this structural proposal. It must be remembered that schools have to be built, not merely to house *x* pupils but to include, in usable terms, y equipment. Limitation of space can limit equipment and so limit education facilities.

How, then, can all three parties, government, local authorities and teachers, work together for the common good? The government is harnessed to the national purse strings. It should, therefore, both encourage and initiate consortia in school design and building. It should give clear guidance as to centralisation policies. And it should be realistic in its curricular recommendations and not ask of schools what they have not the accommodation to provide.

Local authorities should set up planning teams and consult professional opinion as to policies. They should provide for the closest cooperation between architects and schools, so that both architects and teachers can think of education structurally.

Teachers must learn to seek the best for education within the realistic terms of finance available. They may, and it is right that they should, have their dream schools, but they must establish priorities for what is attainable and think of schools, not merely specialist departments.

We have come quite far along this road already, but we should like to see clear signposts and intelligent traffic control.

19

Educational Technology

In a technological age it is both right and inevitable that such technological advance should be reflected in the schools. And, just as workers feel their interests and status threatened by technological advance, so also do many members of the teaching profession. Our modern Luddites may not smash machines today, but they may decry them, reject them blindly, or, more insidiously impede their effective use.

There is little of this attitude in the vocationally biased areas of school instruction. Here there is an increasing demand for more and more up-to-date equipment. Indeed, such departments as commerce, engineering and domestic science frequently provide pupils with equipment and standards which they will seek in vain outside the larger industrial centres. In science departments, too, notably in physics, there is an urgent drive for equipment to promote the new curriculum, and the proper equipping of science laboratories is a constant worry to headmasters and local authorities. Here, if anywhere, poor equipment can mean poor educational opportunity, although there are means to deploy minimum provision before large pupil audiences.

It is when technological advance enters the actual teaching process that we meet a confusion of views and practices. Language teachers naturally welcome the use of tape-recorders, but are all too often alarmed by the intricacies of language laboratories. Where such laboratories are in use they are often regarded as an aid rather than a medium. Such complex equipment has not yet been subjected to controlled experimental use to define its effectiveness. When this obvious task has been tackled we can expect a greatly improved use of such equipment.

Programmed learning must be, to the educationist, an entirely acceptable and efficient means of instruction. But the situation has been complicated by the introduction of programmed learning machines about which the day school teacher quite often expresses doubts. Such machines have been shown at their most effective in industrial training, in commerce and in H.M. Forces. Within the schools it seems necessary, first of all, that teachers should themselves programme their instruction. They should then measure by controlled experiments, the effectiveness of such programmes and work gradually towards the most efficient. When this stage is reached, the mechanical presentation can be acceptably evolved. While some teachers reject machine teaching, others all too readily express an untutored enthusiasm for machines.

Tape-recorders are one of the most acceptable mechanical aids. They are of the greatest value in language, both native and foreign, in music, in drama, and in making available, in terms of complete timetabling flexibility, educational broadcasts. It has taken a long time to convince language teachers of the paramount importance of the spoken word. Too many written examinations have darkened all our yesterdays. In English, too, we have tended to produce, notably in schools of restricted social advantages, literate inarticulates.

Films and slides have long had an honoured and useful place in education, but the means of projecting them are too often in short supply. This limitation is again to be solved by timetabling, that panacea for all scarce and expensive equipment. The position is further aggravated when restriction on projectors and tape-recorders is in contrast to generous expenditure on books and stationery. No one would deny the view that the book has been and remains the chief teaching aid, but its importance has been diminished. In progressive subjects books become readily outdated and, until new loose-leaf texts, capable of continuous amendment are evolved, books must be increasingly aided by other educational media.

By far the greatest source of external social influence and

information in most homes today is, of course, television. And this medium has readily recognised, in national and commercial networks, its educational potential. Even those who decry the influence of television on the young by so doing admit its educational effectiveness. The quality and range of educational television programmes as broadcast by the BBC and ITV have encouraged the installation of CCTV networks by universities, colleges, education authorities and schools. Realising that national networks cannot meet continual specialist needs, such bodies have set about making their own provision. The most ambitious private network in Britain is that now in operation under the Glasgow Education Authority.

Two limiting factors have, of course, restricted this technological expansion. The first has been financial, as such schemes are expensive. The second has been teacher attitudes where many have seen television teaching as a threat to teacher status and as an excuse to avoid the provision of an adequate teaching force. Perhaps a further caveat has been entered by the pioneering enthusiasm of school television promoters, who have been unduly impatient in their attitude to financial strictures and the attitude of the old guard of teachers.

A cool look at the use of television teaching is necessary. Such teaching becomes cheaper in proportion to the number of pupil viewing hours attained. Therefore small schemes, while often highly effective, are also highly expensive. Unless we are to standardise timetables and educational aims, programmes broadcast must be acceptable to the recipients and available when required. Programmes, therefore, must be agreed in content and quality by teacher panels drawn from the given area, and be presented by teachers who take the greatest pains to use this medium well. Each lesson, in fact, should be the best possible lesson. The problem of the availability of broadcasts against varying timetables can be met by video-tape recording facilities.

What of television in relation to the teacher? The teacher presenting a lesson must increase his efficiency and quality, as this medium is merciless and exaggerates both good qualities and weaknesses. A teacher so employed could justly expect increased remuneration, both for his preparation and for the audience reached. Television cannot replace class and laboratory teaching where the practical involvement of students is essential. But television can demonstrate, lecture and illustrate with great efficiency, and can use scarce equipment to reach large audiences.

Those of us in education must not only live with this but must accept the new opportunity and strive for its expansion and efficiency. Teachers cannot and should not base their claims to status and remuneration on scarcity but on quality. Scarcity can be solved, usually by dilution, but for quality all must struggle and strive. The marriage of television teaching and programmed learning is most desirable, and it is a task for the highly skilled professional, conducting his lessons in terms of controlled research and endless improvement.

Educational technology is not, in short, a threat to the teaching profession; it is, rather, another field of greater opportunity. It may change the teaching task, but the change is more challenging and exacting than any so far introduced. We may not all like the increasing speed of change in education, but we must live with it or perish. Calculator arithmetic and computer mathematics are not a new burden, they are a current need. Of all professions that of teaching must be contemporary or fail in its function.

20

Values in Education

So much change, happening and projected, is occurring within our educational system, that we may appear to have lost those values which, in great measure, inspired education during the first half of the century. Then men strove for sound education, within a static and sometimes outmoded pattern, a sense of duty, and the acceptance of the Christian ethic and Christian creed. There was a great emphasis on tradition and a feeling, however illusory, of continuity in standards.

Now education has little imperial relevance, and is urged to regard itself as an instrument of social justice. Duty is now defined as responsible involvement within the community and, while the Christian ethic remains the basis of moral instruction there is little emphasis on Christian doctrine. The examinations, still held in England, in religious knowledge, do not seem to inspire widespread religious enthusiasm or practice, although there is a movement in Scotland directed towards setting up religious knowledge as an examinable subject. This Scottish aim may or may not be desirable, but one is scarcely encouraged by the defence of its protagonists, who urge that children should at least know what they appear likely to reject. There is little feeling in current society for tradition and this is reflected in the strictly contemporary attitude of many schools.

Education, too, is urged to cooperate more and more closely with industry, with the obvious and desirable aim of producing suitable recruits for industrial expansion. Whether liaison with industry will give new and desirable values to school pupils is another matter. It may indeed throw into sharp and disquieting contrast the standards expected of school pupils and those practised by adults. For example, the student is urged to work harder and study more to improve himself and make himself of more service to the community. In industry he finds that extended personal effort expects, at least generally, immediate material reward. Again, a pupil absent without excuse from school is a truant, while an adult absent from his industrial task is simply an absentee. In such circumstances it would appear that the industrial worker has more to learn from the pupil than has the pupil from his older brother in industry. The interaction of industrial and educational attitudes has given a new complexion to the student body at our universities and, indeed, has sometimes tended to produce teachers who themselves give a newer and more mundane interpretation to professional standards.

Can the school be an instrument of social justice? Within its own walls it can, of course, give opportunity, justice and compassion to all. It can inculcate values involving truthful and honest dealing, and promote the Christian ideal of brotherly love and service to the community. But there are challenges which the school cannot meet. It deploys its resources against endless advantages and disadvantages stemming from the varied social backgrounds of its pupils. By day the school can help the deprived, it can, beyond school, help them still further, but the influence of the home, good or bad, remains of paramount strength.

There are those who believe that democratic education involves the belief that all children are equal. They are equal as human beings, in their right to respect, dignity, and to the best education they can absorb. But, given those equalities, the end result inevitably shows a cross-section of humanity, ranging across the ability scatter from the very able to those of limited gifts, and, if education has done its honest best for all, it has discharged its duty. This is not to say that education does succeed in doing its best for all. It has been and remains overconscious of examination success: it has deployed its best against the best, has helped skilfully the intellectually backward, but has, all too often, failed in its responsibilities to the 60 per cent average pupils. We have employed mechanisms in selection and in examinations which, aiming understandably at the proper exploitation of high ability, have led to a sense of aimlessness and underprivilege among the more numerous average.

The sense of proper involvement in society, with due compassion and care for the afflicted and unfortunate, is generally accepted as an educational aim. It tends, however, to be accepted within the terms of general benevolence. Social work is encouraged, if it does not interfere with examinations. There is concentration, too, on the aged and the sick, on specific damaging illnesses and on causes, such as famine relief. All are worthy and deserving areas of activity, but involvement with humanity should mean much more. Children need to be instructed in the interdependence and interrelation of all human endeavour, both social and industrial, in our modern community. They must see society as a body, and see their future as members of that body, with both rights and duties, and with grave responsibilities. Without this most necessary value it would appear that democracy, which is its political expression, may collapse.

The position of religion in the schools has led to their being singled out for adverse comment. The generalisation has been made that less and less attention has been given to religious instruction and to the promotion of the Christian ideal. If this be so, and many would contend that it is not, one could counter with the comment that schools are simply reflecting the gross materialism of the permissive society which they serve.

What is the actual position in schools? The promotion of Christian teaching is protected by government regulation. Parents have a right which they seldom exercise, to withdraw their children from such instruction, even though great numbers are not themselves practising Christians and do nothing to reinforce Christian teaching given by schools. Teachers are permitted to decline to give religious instruction if this is contrary to their personal beliefs. Few exercise this right, fearing, perhaps, somewhat unforgiving reactions from employers, in whose councils the Churches are represented. Among the pupils themselves there has been, in recent years, a great proliferation of exclusive sects, affording an excellent opportunity for Christian tolerance, but little for a sound consensus curriculum. Specialists in religious instruction and visiting chaplains have been increasingly employed. They have done excellent work and shown great dedication but religion is now intensely personal and all committed Christians have a point of view, which, in its honest self, can cause discord. Some schools enjoy the services of full-time chaplains as staff members. Their opportunity is great, as they can live with their charges and bear Christian witness without over-emphasis on preaching and lecturing.

The need for Christian values was never greater in the face of the growing brutality of human behaviour and of daily life and relationships. The restlessness, unhappiness and obvious tragedy of wide sections of youth is a reflection of a lack of idealism and of self-dedication. Churches are right in seeing schools as the area of opportunity. It is there that children can be given what so many of their elders have rejected. But, if this is to be given in terms of history, of doctrinal differences and of examinations, youth may well turn away. In an age of strictly contemporary attitudes, religion must emphasise its relevance to current problems, and must evade no issues. Christ Himself spoke at the roadside and in the marketplace. If His challenge is to be presented and met it must be heard again at work and at play. Values may change in their definition, but we confide that the eternal verities remain.

21

Experiment and Research in Education

The terms 'experiment' and 'research' are widely and inaccurately used in educational circles, a fact bitterly resented by genuine research workers. Both terms are, in degree, related. An experiment has been reasonably defined as 'an action or operation undertaken in order to discover something unknown, to test a hypothesis, or to establish or illustrate some known truth'. Research, on the other hand, is perhaps best designated as 'a course of critical or scientific inquiry'.

The teacher or educationist may conduct, within quite limited circumstances, an experiment. This initial work may be followed by further experiments, whose joint findings lead to a hypothesis. Should this hypothesis merit extensive study it can then become the subject of research. Such research may well involve the careful preparation of experimental material, the use of control groups for comparative study, and the statistical analysis of results attained over a wide field. Even then, the report may indicate no more than a trend or closely defined comparative results.

Educational research has made and is making great contributions to teaching practice and to study. Yet it is fair to say that social, industrial and political views lay a much heavier imprint on educational patterns. Research work often tends to follow rather than precede policies in education. Thus, to the class teacher, research often appears to lack relevance to the current issues and changes which he has to face.

In certain circumstances it appears extremely difficult to mount research. Let us take, for example, that cracked bone of contention, the comprehensive school. If such schools are to be measured for their effectiveness against grammar schools, we must, in a given area, close the grammar schools and set up comprehensives. Comprehensive schools which serve an area in which grammar schools cream off pupils, are not, in fact, comprehensive at all. Again, what comparative study is to be made? It must surely be between a series of age groups housed in a grammar school/secondary modern complex, and similar age groups being educated in six-year comprehensives. It would be desirable, too, to seek reasonable parity in staffing and equipment, and in the social ranking of the areas compared. Lastly, what are our terms of reference? Do we compare academic results, group by group, attained in like curricula, or do we seek to go beyond this and examine social consequences and attitudes?

When we view such a degree of complexity, it is little wonder that research can arrive belatedly to examine the consequences of action already taken. Research, too, in an understandable desire for a sound scientific basis insists on clear terms of reference. Within those terms of reference it applies statistical and objective methods to further its exploration and give validity to its results. But what in terms of general education is valid? Research can and has produced test batteries for entry to courses of higher education. And their selection has proved reasonably accurate. But this selection has accepted a tradition and empirical definition of ability—ability to pass certain ultimate examination targets. Research does not, and perhaps cannot take into account the side effects of selection techniques which it evolves for known specific purposes. There may be, indeed are, types of high ability which it has to ignore. There are social consequences of any test system which it must ignore, but which can gather such strength as to destroy a research-based examination system, as witness the disappearance of the eleven plus in England and twelve plus in Scotland. These examinations were designed to grade pupils for secondary courses in terms of likely success. They were never so viewed by parents, who saw them simply as the strait gate and narrow way to a grammar or high school education, in short, as an entry into an area of privilege. The public and sometimes professional attitude to the secondary modern and junior secondary schools fully confirmed this view. And yet the research done to mount the tests was conducted with entire validity and integrity—within the given terms of reference.

Current statistical methods in educational research are held in varying esteem by teachers. The reason for this is the insistence by the statistician on objective testing, which matches mathematical and scientific subjects far more readily than subjective subjects, such as employ the essay-type answer and accept rational opinion or taste as a correct answer. Certainly the essay-type answer can deploy finer judgments than those available within multiple answer choices. To many teachers the 'right answer' type of question is anathema, as tending to force an unwilling subject into a statistical straitjacket. These, of course, are extreme views, and there is a place for both types of question and answer in research.

Yet another area of teacher complaint is that research, quite rightly, concentrates its resources largely on fundamental educational problems. The teacher, on the other hand, may find himself using outmoded test material, while tests, once valid, await revision. It is only fair to add that the resources available for educational research are very limited, particularly when compared with monies available in America and certain European countries.

Certain fields, too, await cultivation. For example, there is much scope for work in further education and within the sphere of the industrial training boards. Here, again, expansion has heavily preceded research and planning.

The teaching profession is itself insufficiently research minded. Many causes contribute to this. Teachers are, generally, over-employed in the task of teaching, preparing and correcting. They have to meet, increasingly, the demands of new curricula, and to undergo in-service training to keep themselves abreast of change. And yet it is at this very time of change that organised research activities could be most helpful. Local authorities could profitably set up organisations and make finance available for projects approved and controlled by central research councils.

Research, too, is international, as of course it must be, yet an examination of research projects shows a measure of wasteful duplication. In areas where funds are plentiful research can often start before the chosen area has been sufficiently widely developed to ensure valid results. A notable example of this has been in the field of CCTV, where there has too often been a rush into print on the basis of experiments rather than research projects. Many publications on linguistics, too, provide a heady wine without much body.

One must be grateful to those who have laboured long and in restricted circumstances in the field of educational research. And yet, were their desks clear tomorrow they are insufficient in number and underendowed to meet all the educational tasks clamouring for investigation and rationalisation. Teachers, over the next decade, seem likely to have to rethink their contribution to education and their specific task as teachers. They could attempt this task more meaningfully if they shared, however humbly, in opening up the fields of research lying before them. Such a task might involve a real change of emphasis in teacher training. If so, it is a change perhaps overdue. Any move to make teachers question their tasks and check their validity would greatly improve education in terms of relevance to pupil needs.

22

Teaching as a Career

Charles II once spoke of the Royal Navy in the following terms: 'It is upon the navy, under the providence of God, that the safety, honour, and welfare of this realm do chiefly attend.'

In our time of current decline, when we are struggling for existence in terms of industrial and scientific expansion, it might not be thought pretentious to substitute 'education' for 'the navy'. Let there be no mistake, we shall stand or fall by the quality of our education and by the sense of purpose which we instil or fail to instil into the pupils in our charge.

Against such a challenge, how does teaching stand as a career? The teaching force is inadequate, its social and economic status has diminished, and it is fighting an apparently losing battle to meet expanding tasks. The impasse seems to be that we need many more and better qualified teachers just when we cannot or will not afford them. All depends on teachers in the long run, and we are, perhaps, overconscious that we can depend only on ourselves. To the public eye, moreover, we present a picture of disarray, where frustration finds its outlet in internecine war, as bitter as it is futile.

And yet, how little of those current discontents are reflected in classroom work. The staff-room Ajax, defying not only government lightning but all those of his colleagues who disagree with him, is frequently the most dedicated and considerate of teachers, forgetting all in the absorption of his task. Despite all, teaching remains one of the most interesting and mentally rewarding of occupations. There is no work material like the raw stuff of humanity, no problem so persistently challenging as those presented by eager minds or social problems.

It is, of course, a dangerous task. To be a good teacher a man or woman should be truly adult in surroundings which militate against this. The teacher must avoid the posture of an omniscient dictator when daily temptation invites him to this role. He must be compassionate, but should never wear his compassion on his sleeve. He must, above all, have or acquire a sense of humour, as the only safeguard to a sense of proportion.

The teacher, too, must be outward looking, a real member of adult society. He must find his friends both within and outside the profession, or his vision will be dimmed and reduced. Above all he must, God help him, be an example without being a prig or a hypocrite. And he or she must have or cultivate a sense of vocation, while actively resenting the use of this term to justify underpayment.

When we say all this, we remember that even the ceiling of teacher pay is low and that, in a numerous profession there is, under centralisation, less and less room at the top. Jobs at the top, too, become steadily more difficult and demanding. Early retirement is a cause for genuine concern. There is, it should be remarked, no staff training for even senior headships. It says much for professional standards that the effects of amateurism are seldom apparent.

There is the further irritation that many of the advantages attributed to teaching by the public show a strange ignorance of the teaching task. The short working day is apparent but not real. The five-day week is more often a reality for the critics of teaching than for the teachers themselves. The vacations are badly distributed, as the spring term illness rate shows, and the long summer vacation loses considerable charm without financial resources.

Why, then, do we do it, resent it and love it? The answer is, perhaps, that it is a service and truly involves us, handing out rewards and disappointments in equal share. However high the thinking and plain the living, it has its dignity. One can respect one's job and, if recent opinion polls are to be believed, be respected in it.

It is in basic human and domestic needs that so many teachers feel deprived. Few teachers dislike their work. Rather they are absorbed in it, sometimes overabsorbed to exclude, at least temporarily, domestic worries. Men teachers do not seriously resent hardships for themselves, they resent, rather, the poor figure which they cut as providers. They cannot expect those outside the profession, too many of whom enjoy great prosperity without the encumbrance of learning, to accept their valuation of their own worth.

The teaching lot could be bettered, of course, without economic catastrophe. Centralisation of schools has greatly lessened promoted posts. The new large central schools can offer alternative posts, necessary to their efficiency. Again, after prolonged, successful, but unpromoted teaching, there seems little reason why substantial additional payments should not feature in the future. This would ease strain and frustration in mid-career, when family needs are at their peak.

All the evidence of new demands upon the teaching force indicates that teaching will have to attract recruits of the highest possible calibre. Policies of dilution blind themselves to the facts and could be catastrophic if effected. The modern teacher cannot, as perhaps his predecessor too often did, contemplate his academic attainments and his training and consider himself qualified for a full career in his profession. Either he must keep up with progress in his subjects and in their presentation, or be self-relegated to the ranks of the hopeless. Knowledge rapidly outpaces graduate and college trained recruits and in-service training provision, still inadequate, even when general proves ineffectual to meet new demands. Universities may well have to insist on the return of graduates to ensure the continuing validity of degrees awarded but outdated. In such circumstances a university of the air, using television as has been done in postgraduate medicine, and issuing the necessary reading lists and publications, might do great and all-important work.

The introduction of a further concept may be necessary: that of transferability between teaching and other academically based occupations. This may upset the popular concept of the career teacher, but it would provide recruits who would bridge the gap, too wide by far, between academic instruction and the outside world.

These are dangerous days for the actual teaching task too. New curricula demand careful preparation. Textbooks to meet just the right demand are both expensive and scarce. There comes the temptation to provide classes with handouts on new curricula. These must be subject and ancillary to hard teaching and laboratory practice. No teacher can afford to run correspondence courses and count himself a professional.

Without teachers the university benches will gradually empty. Industry, too, will soon witness a falling quality in its recruits, just at the time when adaptability, transfer and retraining are real industrial issues. Those who reject or despise the teaching task must live with their personal values. We need not envy them, as to do so would be to deny our own faith in education as the supreme contemporary challenge.

The retiring teacher is unlikely to leave accumulated wealth when he dies. But he will leave, to the community, his lifelong contribution to their future wellbeing. If he is esteemed by pupils, parents and colleagues he needs no other honours to grace his efforts or his memory.

23

The Future of Education

The trends which we have examined in preceding chapters point clearly to the immediate future of education, but he would be rash who would speculate beyond the immediate future.

In primary education we shall see, as economics permit, the effecting of the findings of the Plowden Report in England and the New Primary Report in Scotland. There will be a heart-searching period of transition, perhaps some measure of disorder, but the new proposals and methods will settle into new patterns, themselves to be changed by future reformers.

Secondary education will witness the raising of the school leaving age, first in the step already forecast and, as industry re-organises, probably by yet another step in the not too distant future. The comprehensive school will find its place and, no doubt, achieve an efficient pattern more, perhaps, in terms of realities than recommendations.

The examination structure is already ripe for reform. Already the numbers involved in state examinations are creating conditions demanding a new and more workable approach. The school leaving age cannot be raised in terms acceptable to parents without at least the award of gradings on a national standard for *all* pupils. Under existing examination circumstances we have noticed a swing from overspecialisation in England, countered in Scotland by the probability of some limiting of the breadth of presentation practised.

New universities, bringing their new degree concepts and new entry qualifications seem likely to have a liberalising effect on the patterns followed by their elders. But it is from industry's attitudes and needs that still greater changes may come in university provision and practice. The forces demanding such change seem likely, moreover, to have financial teeth.

The concept of what is a suitable academic training for teachers may be subject to change, but it is likely to demand more rather than less, if wise councils prevail. The need to regard academic status as requiring periodic refreshment and modernisation may be belatedly recognised and, at least in specific progressive areas, introduced. The teacher scarcity crisis, as its consequences become increasingly apparent, may move from the realm of speculation into that of public inquiry.

Local authorities will, it is expected, be reorganised in larger areas. This should improve planning, reduce waste, make better educational provision, and secure a better deployment of teachers, if the new administrations are really effective. It may be increasingly borne upon such administrations that they must involve the teaching profession increasingly in planning and reform. Without this, larger local government areas could repeat the follies of the past on a larger scale.

There may be a harder time ahead for pupils leaving school as our struggle towards solvency bites ever more deeply into a false affluence. This could mean a more ready consciousness of involvement in the national effort. It might, indeed, limit the tendency to demonstrate and enhance the desire to improve productivity. Recruits to industry must be informed of the need for adaptability for changing occupation, for readiness to accept retraining. The prospect of a job for a lifetime may have little reality for the future school-leaver.

At government level power may change and rechange hands, but those governing must face, according to their varying priorities, largely the same problems. Education remains a basic need and its improvement and reform are vital to national survival. Those in education must see their hopes set against overall national needs and resources, but this does not mean that they should fail to press for a share of those resources commensurate with the importance of their task. Economic difficulties mean the clear assessment of priorities, and the adequate education of the young must surely merit a high degree of priority.

The teacher of the future may expect under existing circumstances and within comprehensive education, a greater social responsibility. He must accept the continuous refurbishing of his own education and skills and the need for the better deployment of his professional gifts. The potential of the technological aids to teaching must be the subject of proper research and, when their areas of genuine contribution are defined, be welcomed and generously provided. The programming of learning is likely to be a growing and most influential element in teaching technique and to form an increasing element in teacher training.

We are now at the inception of a great and continuing building programme which must modernise old schools and build new within the terms of modern education. It is our most earnest hope that, whatever financial restrictions may be necessary, full and continuous consultation with teachers will be a feature of future planning. Both to avoid waste and secure maximum efficiency this is essential.

Parental interest in education, always strong, is likely to grow and it must be the task of educationists to ensure that this is an informed interest. It is in the best interest of both pupils and teachers that parents should have a thorough knowledge of the benefits and limitations of state education. A properly informed electorate is the best safeguard against educational neglect and is likely to be more effective in securing reform than are teachers, always suspect as professionally committed.

There is and will be much complaint regarding changes in education. To such criticism, often based on mental laziness or indifference, it must be made clear that, in an era of rapid change and expanding knowledge, static education would be meaningless. If changes stand the test of relevance to current needs and conditions, they must be welcomed. There is no doubt that sometimes frivolous changes do occur, but their brief existence is well known.

We all, under present difficulties, are engaged in one all-important task, the search for a new Britain, solvent and industrially progressive. Use education to achieve this, and the desired enrichment of living becomes possible. If we fail in this we fail in everything. We can but hope that the necessary vision may be shown in the days ahead.